THE YORKSHIRE BOOK OF THE BED

Edited by

Ian Clayton and Jill Brown

Yorkshire Art Circus
1991

Published by Yorkshire Art Circus,
School Lane, Glass Houghton,
Castleford, West Yorkshire WF10 4QH
Telephone (0977) 550401

© Yorkshire Art Circus
© Cover design: Tadpole Graphics
© Photographs: Terry Cryer, Val Green, Kevin Reynolds,
    Stephen McClarence, Groundwork Trust,
    Pontefract and Castleford Express

ISBN 0 947780 71 9

Classification: General Interest/Humour

Typsetting by Print Assist, Castleford
Printed by Thornton and Pearson Ltd.
Rosse Street, Thornton Road, Bradford BD8 9AS

Yorkshire Art Circus is a unique book publisher. We link our books with performances and offer workshops for first time writers. Yorkshire Art Circus projects have successfully toured community centres, colleges, galleries, clubs and art centres. In all our work we bring new artists to new audiences.

For details of our programme of workshops, performances and exhibitions send for our brochure and book list at the address above.

Yorkshire Art Circus is a non-profit making limited company, currently seeking charitable status.

We would like to thank the following organisations for their involvement in this book:

Bradford Library
The College of Ripon & York St John
Duravend, Jiffy Condom Factory, South Kirkby
Featherstone Carpets & Furnishings

We would like to thank the following people and organisations for the use of their photographs:

Terry Cryer   Stephen McClarence
Val Green   Groundwork Trust
Kevin Reynolds   Pontefract and Castleford Express

We would like to thank the following organisations for support towards this project:

CONTENTS

4

We would like to thank the following people who have contributed to this book:

Rachel Adam
Ginette Ainsley
Ghazala Alavi
Pam Auty
Paul Barton
Mrs Beckwith
Beryl Berry
Lyn Bowley
Rose Brent
Gerald Brown
Georgina Brown
Jill Brown
Richard Brown
Sue Brown
Anne Bullen
Philip Carr
Mary Cassidy
Gladys Chapman
Ken Churm
Margaret Churm
Rachel Clark
Tony Clayton
G Clough
Janet Colbeck
Sheila Coll
Rita Cooper
Leonard Couzens
Kate Cozens
Terry Cryer
Richard Daggett
Kath Dalton
Pam Davenport
Steve Davenport
Glen Davis
Tina Davis
Chris Denobrica
Tommy Dermody
Pat Dickenson
Mark Duggan
Frank Duncan
Joanne Durrant
Audrey Earnshaw
Su Enefer
Ken Enelson
Kathleen Exley
Denis Fearnley
Hilda Fletcher
Olive Fowler

Patricia Frederiksen
Jill Freeman
Ronald Fryatt
Jonathan Gallimore
Melanie Garrett
John Gaukroger
John Gummerson
Audrey Haggerty
Terry Haggerty
Katharine Hague
Pat Hall
Theresa Hardman
Majorie Harwood
Annette Hayes
Fred Hayes
Tracey Paris Hewett
Mandy Hibbins
Eleanor Hill
Nick Hill
Rebecca Hoddle
David Hodgson
Theresa Hughes
Annette Hyer
Clare Jenkins
Albert Jukes
Matt Kenway
Keely Knights
Bill Lang
David Lathan
Terry Laycock
Doreen Lee
Brian Lewis
Jacob Lewis
Jessica Lewis
Alice Longley
M Lonsdale
Beverley Lumb
Tony Lumb
Sally Lund
Iris Marshall
Catherine MacKenzie
David McAndrew
Victoria McBride
Sarah McGilloway
Joan McSwiney
Louise Mason
Nicola Mellor
Catherine Morris

Christine Mortimer
Neil Mortimer
Enid Murgatroyd
Jayne Murphy
Beatrice Naday
Anjana Narine
Mary Anne Neary
Linda Nievwenhuis
Doreen O'Kelly
Jean Oldfield
Philip O'Readan
Freda Owens
Phil Paver
Bill Payne
Mary Payne
Benjamin Pearson
Elsie Pearson
Pamela Pennock
Mark Perry
Madelaine Peskett
Catherine Pidd
Margaret Pilkington
Denise Probert
Wagar Rashmid
Sue Readman
M Reeve
Rabia Rehuyan
Diane Robson
Joyce Rogers
Mark Lowther Ross
Lizzy Ryan
Michael Sailor
M Sanderson
Chris Saunders
Marilyn Saunders
Reini Schühle
Catherine Shaw
Gwen Sheriff
Hilary Shields
Caroline Sketton
Ian Smith
Michael Stevens
Mark Sturrock
I Roper
Jo Ruff
Alwyne Sanderson
Melanie Sheerin
Helen Small
Jean Smith
Margaret Smith

Paul Southern
Janet Spears
Esme Spence
Jennifer Stead
Barbara Stewart
Alison Stogden
Violet Stogden
Liz Stringer
Kate Taylor
Christine Taylor
Steve Taylor
Vina Thaker
Cliff Toft
Mahala Townsend
Della Trueman
Rachel Van Riel
Richard Van Riel
Amy Vaughan
Joe Vickery
Darby Walsh
Josie Walsh
Elsie Ward
Celia Watson
Linda Watson
Mandy Webb
Lillian Whiteley
G Whitney
Margaret Whitton
Jane Wilcox
David Wilson
Derek Wilson
Gavin Wilson
Ingrid Wilson
Michael Wilson
Eileen Wood
Mohammed Younis

Editorial Team:

Jill Brown
Tina Davies
Audrey Haggerty
Beverley Lumb
Tony Lumb
Phil Paver
Alison Stogden
Rachel Van Riel
Lillian Whiteley

INTRODUCTION

This book was conceived on the back seat of a Ford Cortina travelling at speed to Barnsley. Yorkshire Art Circus was running a writing day with the Royston Women writers, a group who first came together during the Miners' Strike.

My colleague that day suggested, 'Let's do something a bit more exciting than normal — I'm fed up with doing books on Housing and Environment.'

'Like what?' I responded.

'Let's do Love, Lust and Divorce in Barnsley.'

I thought that we couldn't do that with a group of people we hardly knew.

'Beds' was the theme we decided upon. The greater themes of birth, death and lovemaking would all tie into it. When you think about it you spend a third of your life in bed.

The writing day was a great success. One woman told the story which opens this book while another told the one about sleeping on a plank when she worked with a travelling show. The Yorkshire Book of the Bed was born that evening. We sat admiring it laid on a table in a public house.

We applied the same model for a writing workshop with students at The University College of Ripon and York St. John. The Ripon Book of the Bed fed back into the mother book.

We then moved the project on to the Arts and Industrial complex at Dean Clough, Halifax. The collection of tales there took the form of verbal storytelling and writing in response to set writing exercises. We toured hospitals, old people's homes and Technology Centres using the same techniques. At Bradford Library we interviewed staff and library users with a team of students from the Art Circus University of Talk. Our journey ended at a condom factory in West Yorkshire.

The Book of the Bed is a collection of stories about beds. It is a funny book, a sad book and also an educational book. The editorial team are all members of the University of Talk, a new initiative in education run jointly by Wakefield MDC and Yorkshire Art Circus. The students of the University of Talk are storytellers and writers who are improving their technique by working in practical situations like the day we went story gathering at Bradford. Our motto is that 'Everyone has a story to tell, when you ask the right questions.'

And so to bed. If ever there was a book for bedtime, you're holding it.

Ian Clayton

BEDCLOTHES

Diddle Diddle Dumpling my son John
Went to bed with his trousers on
One shoe off and one shoe on
Diddle Diddle Dumpling my son John

☐ 'Gentle sleep, nature's soft nurse.' This adage was embroidered on a linen nightie case I once owned and the phrase always made me feel dreamy, warm and happy all at once. I have no idea what happened to that piece of embroidery but somewhere I am sure it still exists in somebody's book of treasured sayings. Beds, like fashion, have changed but basically they all serve the same purpose. The old, ornately painted, iron bedsteads, which were the pride and joy of our mothers, were further enhanced by the addition of a gigantic feather bed and drapes. There is nothing more comfortable. It soothes aching limbs and warms chilled feet without the aid of a hot water bottle.

☐ There you are, you've got your black satin sheets, matching pillow cases and you're wearing all the gear that would send Mary Whitehouse into cardiac arrest for a year. You are ready for your monthly session of conjugal rights. Then in walks your husband, wearing his sexy gear — you know the sort — paisley patterned pyjamas, drawstring waist, of course, and his socks! While he just slumps into bed without a mention about the expensive sheets and the trouble you've taken to look your best, you slide gently in beside him — and surprise, surprise, you are still waiting for his advances fifteen minutes later!

☐ I once went to bed wearing my boyfriend's leather jacket because he'd just lent it to me and it smelt of him.

☐ I can't get away with continental quilts. For me, a properly made bed is a joy to look at; sheets ironed, blankets pulled taut and tucked in tightly. When I get into bed it's all smooth and crisp with no creases to irritate me.

☐ We didn't have the luxury of central heating when we were kids so on cold nights our night attire was very different from what it is now. An old flannelette shirt of Dad's was great to curl your knees up into or a Grandad vest made of lovely warm material. Bed socks were a must. It was so cold sometimes icy patterns formed on the inside of the bedroom window. An old coat or a rug came in handy to put on the bed. Sleeping with my two sisters helped a lot too. We kept each other warm.

☐ The first house we had after we were married was an old council house. We moved in in the middle of winter and it was freezing. I went to bed in a pom-pom cap, bed socks, gloves, nightie and cardigan. I enjoy reading in bed but I couldn't turn the pages wearing gloves. My husband stripped off and jumped into bed starkers. He said I was nesh.

☐ I'd never go to sleep in the dark when I was little. I was always scared. My sister and I shared a room and we would pull back one curtain each in the morning.
Once I pulled back mine but she wouldn't

pull back hers. A huge moth flew out and I ran out screaming. My sister followed me into my brother's room and he also ran out screaming. We all ran through to my Grandad's room still screaming. By this time he'd got up and was stood in his nightshirt with his walking stick not knowing what was going on.

☐   Can you remember brushed nylon nighties? I couldn't understand why they put the fluffy side on the outside so I always wore mine inside out. Then there were nylon sheets. What with the nightie and the sheets together, when I turned over, there were sparks coming off the bed.

☐   Ours was a big iron framed bed with brass knobs on each corner. Three of us slept in it when we were kids. There was an old army coat hanging on the back of the bedroom door and, when it was cold, we would use it as an extra cover. One night Mam called upstairs, 'What's all the noise?'

I answered, 'It's our Tommy, Mam, he's pulling the coat about.'

'It's not a coat,' Mam said, 'it's an eiderdown. Your aunty's here.'

After a while she called up again. 'What are you doing now?'

'It's him again, Mam. He's pulled the sleeve out of the eiderdown.'

Robin and Richard,

Were two pretty men.

They lay in bed

Till the clock struck ten.

Then up starts Robin,

And looks at the sky.

Oh, brother Richard,

The sun's very high.

☐   Possibly the roughest man I've ever been to bed with was a greasy old motorbiker called Bert. When I think about it we did a lot of things together. I travelled behind him as a pillion passenger on countless tours, we were labourers on the same building site in Leeds, we drank pints and pints of beer in pubs all over Yorkshire — we once did 26 pints apiece in a day at Beverley — and we used to go camping regularly. So I suppose sharing the same bed was quite normal. Except that he rarely took his motorbike jacket off and he talked a lot. The reason we shared a bed was simple. Almost every weekend when he was single we had parties at a shared house. I had just a mattress on a bare board bedroom floor so those who wanted to sleep either kipped on the boards or on the mattress with me.

☐   I'm told this is true but it could, I suppose, be one of these urban myths you hear about. The woman who told it to me was a deputy headteacher in Doncaster and she said that it happened to a boy she and her daughter knew.

He was about nineteen, heterosexual; an Air Force mechanic and very straight on the surface but given to dressing himself in women's underclothes. One night when he and his girlfriend were playing around, he borrowed her gear, brought out some washing line and persuaded her to tie him to the bed ends. I don't know why it happened, if there was an argument, if it was devilment, disgust or what but instead of letting him go, she walked out. He was there all night. It wasn't particularly cold but cold enough. He cried a lot. On the teatime on the Saturday, after the pubs had closed, she returned with two friends and later that night the police arrived to free him.

☐   My husband is partial to suspenders and stockings in bed. I suggested that this was a form of bondage and why did men feel they were exempt from doing something similar to turn women on? The next night he lay on the bed with his socks on and I said, 'What on earth are you doing?'

'Well,' he said, 'you seem to think I should dress up for you. Sorry I haven't got a pair of suspenders to go with them.'

Val Green

When my brother and I were small we used to put on pairs of our mum's best silk gloves and would bounce about on the bed pretending to be boxers. This particular day we were bouncing about and I was propelled forward by one of those big heavy springs which formed the base of the bed and landed my chin square on our Des's fist. I was out cold for a few seconds and when I came round he was stood over me with his hands held above his head as though he had just knocked out Sonny Liston.

The first occasion when I can recall being embarrassed was during a holiday visit to our cousins. We'd had our hands and faces washed and were in our pyjamas ready for bed, four of us in drawstring waist ones with open flyholes. 'I can see his gun sticking out!' shouted cousin Gary and they all looked at me.

Old Boniface he loved good cheer,
And took his glass of Burton,
And when the nights grew sultry hot
He slept without a shirt on

When central heating came along and I grew older and became too fat, I always slept in the nude simply for comfort. It was too hot to wear pyjamas. One morning at about 1.30 am we were wakened by a hullabaloo in the street. Our next-door-but-one neighbour, a young idiot who lived on his own, had come home drunk as usual. He had put some food on the cooker, gone to the toilet and fallen asleep. Before long the house was blazing away like a bonfire and soon the fire brigade was clanging its way to the scene. Me and the wife leapt out of bed and opened a window to find all the street either outside or leaning out of a bedroom window.

'Throw us a blanket,' a young lass shouted at me, 'he's on fire.'

'Let the silly bugger burn,' I said, dodging back into the bedroom. I didn't see why I should waste my time on a menace to the community.

After a short while I leaned out again to see what was going on. The fire brigade had everything under control. As I leaned further out of the window, I heard a slight sizzle and almost simultaneously felt a sharp pain. I leapt back into the bedroom and only then realised that being naked, I had burnt the end of my willie on the hot radiator. That's what I got for being nosy.

☐   'How to undress in front of your husband' was the headline on my favourite weekly journal. The year was about 1950. The cover featured a sheet of Poly-photos of a very beautiful woman. The first photograph showed her fully clothed and each subsequent shot was of the woman at various stages of undress, posturing in a very

seductive manner. The accompanying article within the pages of the journal dramatised the actions of each of the photographs. It was a surprisingly daring feature for its time but I suppose in those early post-war years a lot of people suffered from repressed sexuality and pieces like that helped them.

☐   My dad, a pensioner, asked me if I could guess what Stan, one of his friends, had given him for Christmas. I said that I couldn't. 'A call girl,' he announced.

Stan frequented massage parlours and on one of his visits he had paid one of the girls to go round to my parents' house and see my father. My mother had been dead four years.

'She was really nice,' he said. 'Very clean, not an old bag.'

I wasn't shocked but I was surprised. When I tried to project the image into my mind, I saw him lying on the bed in one of his old floppy vests and her sitting beside him in pure white underclothes. There was no sexual activity, they were just sitting there talking. I didn't know if she was blonde, brunette or what. I didn't know if he kept his glasses on. In fact, the only thing which was real was my mother's candlewick bedspread.

☐   When I pop my clogs, I hope it's here in bed; in decent dignity with my old hot water bottle.

☐   I used to have a luminous, pink, furry, elephant water bottle called Nelly. I wouldn't go to bed without it even when it was hot weather. When I was about six, I fell asleep clutching hold of her only to wake drenched to the skin. First I thought I had wet the bed. Then I realised that Nelly was a funny flat shape. I ran out of the bedroom yelling that Nelly had been killed and all her insides had come out.

☐   We had an old fashioned fireplace when I was a girl and the shelves from the oven were taken out and wrapped in cloths and put in our beds to warm them up. That was before hot water bottles.

Pontefract and Castleford Express

☐ I never had a teddy bear when I was a little girl but I had a special rag doll called Tabitha which my mum made for me; she made up for any teddy bear in the whole world.

☐ I have had two terry nappies since I was four. I suck the thumb on my left hand and smell the nappies. The reason I've got two is because I must smell them when they're cold so I alternate.

☐ My partner introduced the duvet to our house and after a time I had got so used to it that I forgot that we had ever used blankets and sheets. My parents didn't visit us often but after my mother died Dad came on his first visit. In many ways he was a bit hopeless. It was not his fault − he was an only child and had had a doting wife − but he was not the most pratical of men. I showed him up to his room and saw that he knew which was his towel and which was his flannel but never thought to say anything about the bedclothes. I went to bed early that night; I found it difficult talking to him and he to me. The next morning I asked him how he had slept.

'Not well,' was the reply.

'Why?' I asked.

'I was too cold.'

'Don't you like the duvet?'

Then it came out. He hadn't known how to use it. He had undone the press studs, climbed inside and slept on top of the feather duvet. The night had been slept under the equivalent of a thin cotton sheet.

☐ We only had scanty bedclothes in Africa, perhaps just a cotton sheet. When we came to Bradford, we had three or four blankets, quilts, socks, jumpers and trousers and that was in the summer.

☐ I was on a Hospice Arts conference in Hull recently and there were three of us queueing for the ladies' toilet at lunchtime. I peered at the name badge of the woman next to me and tried to make conversation.

'Where are you from?'

'Pontefract.'

'That's amazing. I'm from Pontefract too.'

'Yes,' she said. 'I thought you might be. Your husband's The Man Who Doesn't Wear Pyjamas.'

I had to go in the cubicle then and when I came out she went in and someone else was trying to get past me so I had to go back out to the main room where I was buttonholed by a volunteer from Huddersfield.

Half an hour later I managed to find the woman again.

'What do you mean? The Man Who Doesn't Wear Pyjamas?'

She laughed. She was very confident, smartly dressed and well made up. Not Richard's type at all. I thought of his paunchy body next to hers and realised that he does wear pyjamas now so she must have known him a few years back.

'When I was a student nurse at Pontefract Infirmary,' she said, 'he was brought in as an emergency for a gastroscopy. It turned out to be nothing and he was on his feet next day. He walked everywhere on the ward in this little shorty robe and it caused a scandal. I was only a student so I wasn't so shocked but it went round the hospital in no time − 'There's a man on that ward who doesn't wear pyjamas!' That was in 1977.'   'But that's 13 years ago!'

'It made such an impact I've never forgotten his name and I recognised it on your conference badge just now.'

☐ I always sleep naked. I can't do with clothes on in bed, apart from when my sister comes to stay. She sleeps with me because I've only got one bed. I always keep my knickers on then. Funny thing is she always strips off, even her knickers.

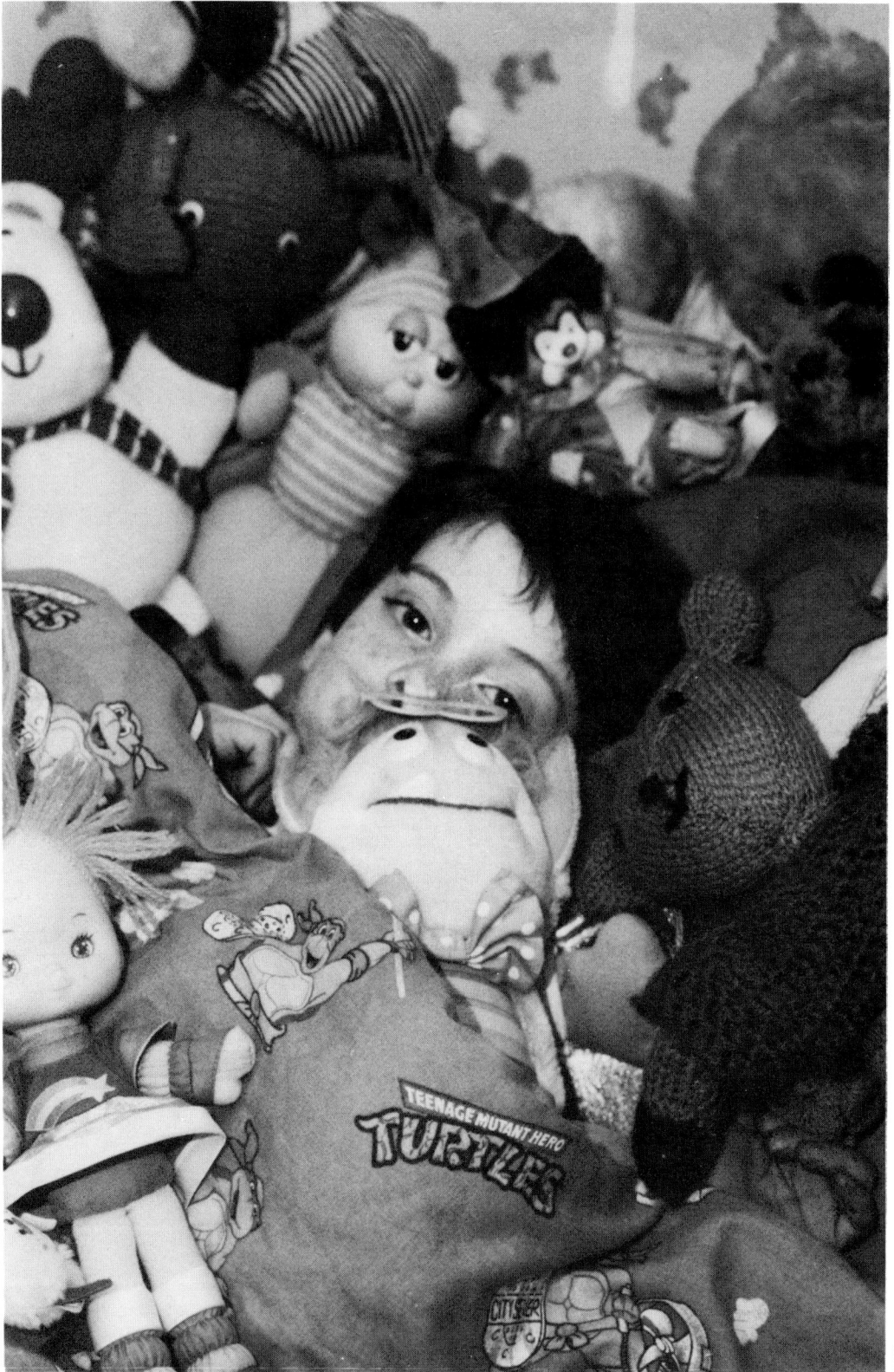

BEDMATES

Goosey, goosey gander,
Whither shall I wander?
Upstairs and downstairs,
And in my lady's chamber.

☐ I don't think about the bedroom as a special place. I know it's always the last to get decorated because it's the one that nobody sees. It's just for sleeping really and for getting ready for going out. I love getting ready. I hang my clothes out, run the bath, mousse my hair and put on my makeup in front of the mirror on the landing. I usually go out with my daughter and her mates so they'll all be getting ready at the same time. It gets a bit hectic dancing in your bra and pants to the cassette player while trying to do your hair but we have some good laughs.

☐ What's in my bedroom is mine and nobody else's. I have all my personal papers in the wardrobe; there's a top flap that comes down. I keep all my personal mementoes and memories there; my dad's medals and my mum's little bits of jewellery, nothing really valuable, just little brooches we gave her when we were small. There's the first sticky picture our Wendy did when she went to nursery. It's got bits of straw on it and they're all curled up. I looked at it the other day and I thought it's a bit disgusting but I keep it. Little silly things mean a lot.
I've got a shoebox with a red ribbon round with all my mum and dad's love letters from the war. There's the first Christmas card he sent after I was born. He couldn't get a card, of course, so he folded up a piece of paper into four and drew on it.

☐ The bed my sister and I shared in the 1940s was an obstacle course. In winter it was littered with stone hot water bottles, bricks and oven sheets and we were pinned down under the dead weight of blankets. We were told that the bedsprings went rusty because of the steam rising from the po in the cold bedroom, so we covered ours with the snakes and ladders board.

☐ I always went into my mother's room each morning before going to school. Each morning, without fail, you could hear snoring from under the duvet. Then the duvet would move and out would come our big white boxer, Scooby, going to get a drink out of the toilet now the door was open.

☐ I've a shelf for antiques and teapots in my bedroom. The bedroom is a special place with my things in more than my husband's, my dresses in the wardrobe, all my bits on the dressing table. My husband doesn't really know what's on my bedroom shelf. I love going to fleamarkets. If I come home with something new and he says, 'Where did you get that?' I'll answer, 'Oh, I've had it for ages!' and put it on my shelf. He's none the wiser.

☐ A good woman friend of mine had a bit of trouble recently so I said she could come down and stay with me. I've only got one big double bed so we slept together. It was quite a good feeling, two women sharing a bed. We felt secure together.

☐ I've got a lot of friends and they often stay. I don't mind if they want to sleep in bed with me. Sleeping together or sharing your bed doesn't have to connect with sex. My bed is not sacred, at least not to friends.

☐   I don't mind sleeping with girlfriends when they stop overnight but men I can't do with. No matter how well you know them, they've always got wandering hands.

☐   A woman friend of mine at college had written in Dymo-tape on the headboard of her bed *I said maybe and that's final!*

> Little Blue Betty lived in a den,
>
> She sold good ale to gentlemen;
>
> Gentlemen came every day,
>
> And little Blue Betty hopped away.
>
> She hopped upstairs to make her bed,
>
> And she tumbled down and broke her head.

☐   My friend's wife bought him a miner's helmet so that he could read in bed. For myself, I've always read there. My first wife hated the habit and if I put my hand on my heart I'd admit that it was one of the things that contributed to the breakup of the marriage. 'Beds are for sleep,' she'd say. My partner now doesn't mind how often the light goes on. She's read with a torch from girlhood.

I say this because if I had to talk about the pleasantest moments I have had in bed I would not dwell on sexual pleasures but on the intellectual ones. I remember once spending a night with an intellectual socialist woman in a posh hotel in Oxford. We made love, or was it lust, and when we had finished and were sitting up taking a cup of tea she asked, 'Where do you stand on Kronstadt?'

I see her on the television occasionally but when I pull her out of my memory and she stands before me, it is not so that I can admire those dimples in what I will call her bum, but I see her posing an intellectual question of great merit which I still do not totally understand.

Terry Cryer

☐ My worst waking up was when his mum first caught us in bed. We hadn't done anything, that's what bugged me. At his mum's he used to sleep in the same bedroom as his younger brother and his mum came in on a morning at 7.30 to get them up. This night I stayed I expected to wake up and be well out of the way before 7.30 but we slept in. When she came in, there I was laid in bed with him in a big long T-shirt.

'If that's all you want my son for....!' she ranted. I was afraid and felt really embarrassed. He wasn't bothered. 'Get out of my bedroom!' he shouted and we could hear her slamming the pots in the kitchen. Then he bolted up the three bolts on the door and went back to bed. I was more embarrassed than he was but she's alright with me now.

☐ I walked out of my marriage in Manchester when I was 29. He was good to the kids but very jealous. I couldn't go anywhere without he wanted to know where I was. Then I started answering him back so he started swiping me. That went on for a few years and then I got fed up. I came to Barnsley to live at my sister's. It was like jumping out of the frying pan into the fire.

It was a bloody awful life. Our Maisie and her husband Bob were rowing every day. I had an idea she was thick with Tommy, a bloke that fancied her, and lodged with them. And it turned out that it was true. This night her husband had gone to work on nights so myself, our Maisie, and Tommy's mate, Jack, went to the club. Tommy and Jack decided to have a shift off from the pit because they had been told that there was a good turn on. Me and our Maisie ended up two bloody good turns that night as well.

We came home from the pub after having a smashing time. I ended up in bed with Jack and our Maisie ended up in bed with Tommy. I think we were all bloody starry-eyed that night but we weren't so bright-eyed next morning.

I nearly pissed myself when I floated down the stairs. Tommy, the lodger, was sat on the sofa. Our Bob sat on a chair. They both had faces like well-slapped arses. Our Maisie was in the kitchen getting some breakfast ready. I went in to her.

'What's up with them two?' I asked.

'What do you think's up with them?' she whispered to me. 'He caught us in bed together.'

'How?' I asked.

'I'll tell you. It seems he had hurt his fingers in the pit and he came home early.'

'Well,' I whispered back, 'the door was locked.'

'I know,' she said, 'but the crafty bloody git got through the window.'

Talk about partners in crime. We both sounded like two bloody croaking frogs. Well, I burst out laughing. I couldn't help it.

'Do you think it's funny, Liza?' Bob said.

'No, it's not funny. I'm laughing at what our Maisie's just said.'

'Oh, are you?' he replied. 'Did she tell you how I found the pair of them like the bloody babes in the wood?'

Well, I let out one yell, I couldn't hold it back. Our Maisie looked at me and she set off laughing.

'I'm going to bed,' he said, 'Cos that one,' meaning me, would laugh if she saw a woman's arse on fire.' With that he banged up the stairs just as Jack was coming down.

'I suppose you've had some bloody slap and tickle as well?'

'Yes,' replied Jack, 'and it was lovely.'

He banged in the bedroom and slammed the door.

'Well, we'll see what's bloody lovely when I get up because you can all get ready to bleeding flit.'

Now don't you think for one minute that this was a regular thing bobbing in and out of bed like two bloody sparrows on a twig. Our Maisie was fed up with her husband and, as I told you what a miserable bugger he was, I don't think there was any love left in their marriage. Well, I know there wasn't and like me, she had to get married. We were nearly forced to get married in our day. We had committed a terrible crime losing our virginity. Look at them in the papers today. They can get a thousand pounds a time for smacking some dirty old bugger arse. In my day, them poor old buggers hawking their duck on Oxford Road in Manchester were lucky if they got half a crown and a bloody Woodbine.

☐ The conflicting demands of sex and sleep are always hard to reconcile. I found it especially difficult at the annual Open University summer school. Everything you've heard about Open University summer schools is true. It's a stimulus to brain and body at the same time — a wonderful break from your ordinary self and your ordinary commitments. People go wild in a buzz of intellectual, social and sexual excitement. Some sit up talking all night and go to classes still bubbling with ideas in the morning. And there's always one couple every class who pair off on the opening Saturday night and aren't seen again till Thursday.

I didn't want to choose between intellectual pleasures and sexual ones. I wanted both. But the problem I found over the years was the bed. Single college beds are narrow. Slim undergraduates can share them quite happily but whenever I had a good sexual experience I paid for it with lack of sleep afterwards. A night spent tossing and turning, alternately crushed up against the wall or dangling your legs in the cold air over the bed edge, was not conducive to mental concentration the next morning.

How could I have my cake and eat it? One year I heard there were just a few double rooms with twin beds in. They usually went to men. How did you get one? Apparently you just asked. Queueing at the registration desk, I decided to risk it.

'Can I have a double room?'

No problem. No-one gave a second glance at a woman asking.

I found the room, did a dance of glee and moved the beds together. This was going to be the best summer school yet.

It turned out to be the worst. The night went well but in the morning I had large red swellings all over my legs — fleabites. I moved out sharpish and spent the rest of the week coping with different itches from usual.

☐ My first marriage bed was a three quarter with a sprung mattress in Portobello, Edinburgh. A long way from my home in West Yorkshire. Eric and I had run away to get married. It was frightening and also exciting.

It started on Thursday night when my parents had gone to babysit at the farm opposite. Eric arrived and helped me with my case and bag to his auntie's house where I stopped the night. We went early on the 6 o'clock bus to Leeds while the streets were quiet. Eric had to go to work to collect his wages and holiday pay and I spent the day window shopping and having my hair done. We caught the overnight train to Edinburgh. Any trepidation I had went through the window as we cuddled up to one another in our compartment.

☐ So there I was in my garret, poring over my studies, away from loved ones, missing him like mad. How should I introduce my first lesson tomorrow?

'Now, girls, today we are all going to draw something we've all got but cannot see without using a mirror'

Oh no! Don't say that! Definitely don't use those words — underline do not. Mmmm but he does have a lovely body — streamlined for smooth action — do not — do not..

Oh, hang this for a game of soldiers. Forget the mirrors. I'm going to lie down and indulge myself.

I said 'indulge' myself — as in think beautiful thoughts! After all, we both agreed we felt there was something in this ESP lark. Perhaps if I think long enough and hard enough we'll make contact. Encircle the globe. Did I say long and hard? Do not, repeat, do not use those words.

If he's thinking beautiful thoughts too, we might, just might, touch minds....

Peep, peep. Oh! shut up. Damn, where is the alarm button?

Irish Billy and Scarlet Lil were on the stairs.

'Good morning! Sleep well you two?'

'Mmmm.'

'So did I, so did I. Well, except..'

'Except what?'

'Well, I thought my bed rocked during the night. Ha, ha, you don't think the foundations of this crumbling old place are crumbling to that extent, do you?'

'We never felt anything. No, not last night anyway,' said he, patting his wife's tum.

This is the eight o'clock news. Parts of North Wales and the Birkenhead area were hit by an earthquake this morning. The tremors were some of the strongest ever recorded in Britain.

☐   All youngsters are inquisitive about how to kiss, the sort of kiss for your first romantic date. I was no exception and it is something me and my friends would talk about and try to understand how to do. We practiced at home, on the mirror, which seems a bit narcissistic looking back, and on our bedroom pillows, trying to get the hang of it. You had an idea about how it should be done but were not quite certain, so the pillow would be subjected to a hard snogging type kiss or a smoochy delicate kiss or any combination in between. Of course, when you kissed you always closed your eyes, especially if it was the mirror.

☐   My initiation into the world of sexual activity happened relatively late in life at 29 and was the result of curiosity rather than any particular lustful interest in the man. He was an old school friend I kept bumping into, who finally asked me out. His intentions towards me were quite apparent and I decided that as long as the offer was there I might as well find out what it was like.

My preparations for the big event were quite dispassionate. After bathing and dressing I tidied the bedroom by throwing discarded clothing into the bottom of the wardrobe and kicking odd shoes under the dressing table. I then straightened the duvet and sat on the bed to apply styling gel and blow dry my hair. I was ready.

The evening went as planned and by 11.00 pm the experiment had begun. My guinea pig proved to be quite athletic and I found myself wanting to laugh at the absurdity of it all. After quite a lot of thrashing about on my bed we lay together relaxing and my partner complained that he was lying on a patch of something sticky. I realised then that my back was also covered in the same sticky substance, which I assumed had come from him. He denied that it had anything to do with him and it was then that I noticed the sweet, coconut fragrance and instantly knew what it was. I had left the open tube of Vidal Sassoon styling gel on the bed and the contents were now spead all over the duvet cover. My partner and I retired, giggling, to the bathroom where he had to sponge me down. Actually, that was the highlight of the evening.

☐   I don't bother much with sex these days. I'd sooner sit up in bed with a lump of pork pie.

☐   There was plenty of hand-sewn Irish linen in the room and a statue of Billy Byrne, one of Horne Tooke's rebellious compatriots outside the bedroom window, so there was no doubt that this was Ireland.

Catholicism dominated Wicklow twenty years ago, possibly it still does. In an age when naked girls were beginning to appear on the front of the British tabloids, the headline in the *Irish Times* on the day we arrived was that a bishop had climbed a Holy Mountain in County Mayo barefoot.

The bed was lumpy but we settled down, had a good laugh about the oddness of the day and eventually got to stroking each other. I was on top.

Then I looked up. Directly above the bed in which we were acting out the critical stage of adultery was a picture of the Virgin Mary. She was dressed in red and blue, her head was tilted slightly to one side and in her hand was a bleeding heart. Drops of blood led down towards the frame.

'Christ,' I said, 'the Pope could patent that as a form of natural contraception.'

☐   I had to prepare a social enquiry report on a lady who was to appear before a court

Kevin Reynolds

to answer a charge of soliciting, to which she had pleaded guilty.

I found the house I required and knocked. The door was open so I went inside to find the right flat. Another knock was answered by a loud 'Come in' and so I did.

The room was quite dim as the curtains were closed. Was this light the well joked about 'red light'?

'Hello, love, are you here to do me report?'

I couldn't at first see where the voice came from but as my eyes became used to the gloom I noticed that the furniture consisted of just a bed and a table. The voice came from the bed. Then I realised that there was another head in the bed, the same bed. That head moved as the lady urged her companion to 'Wait outside a bit, love.'

Taking absolutely no notice of me, the head and its owner arose, grabbed some clothing and left the room.

'Now, love,' she said, patting the bed, 'come and sit down.'

If they bite
Squeeze them tight,
Then they won't come,
Another night.

☐   It nearly drove me out of my head. I think it'd be enough to send anybody crackers, coping with bed bugs. Everything had to be fettled. My friend helped me. We took the hessian from under the mattress, then rubbed all the springs with paraffin so the bugs would run down the legs into it. Eventually we got rid of them, after cleaning bedding, carpets and even treating the floorboards. But for a long time I checked the bed thoroughly every night before I got into it.

☐   Round about 1934 in Lancaster, you could spend a night in a lodging house for fourpence a night. You often got loused up but you were out of the cold.

☐ Next door to our house lived two old men, one a bit younger than the other. I can't remember their relationship but as they grew older they became more and more unhygienic in their ways. Lots of houses had to have the council in to fumigate after a plague of bugs or after someone had an infectious disease. The time came when the two old men died and, as they had no relations, the council came to clear out the house. Living next door, we saw everything.

The council men knocked out the upstairs window at the back and began to throw out all the stuff. Lots of nosy neighbours came to see what the old chaps had. My most glaring recollection was when they threw out the old men's bed. First the bed ends, then the mattress and finally the springs. As the bits hit the ground, a couple of council men were ready with hand sprays to kill off some of the bedbugs which rose into the air in a great cloud. How the old chaps slept in that bed I'll never know. My childish logic thought that the bedbugs were used to them and didn't bite.

☐ When I stayed at my granny's, I used to sleep in a lovely feather bed. Sometimes I had to help Gran to give the bed a real good shake. It was hard work. But the worst job was when it was spring cleaning time and the feather mattress was taken off the bed. All the feathers were taken out and the cover was washed. Then all the feathers were put back in. My granny always said that this was done to prevent fleas getting into the bed.

☐ When I first moved away from home, I rented a furnished flat. It was quite spacious and the rent was reasonable. Although, on the face of it, it looked clean and tidy, it had this sort of atmosphere of squalor. Or maybe it just seems that way retrospectively. It was the first time I'd slept on a bed that wasn't a family one. It had obviously seen a bit of wear but it had a clean, probably new, mattress cover on it. That should have warned me.

I occasionally thought about looking underneath this mattress cover but I decided against it on the basis that I didn't really want to know the truth.

After I had been there a few weeks, I discovered a number of small spots on my arms, chest and legs but at the time I was more concerned with an invasion of small beetles in the kitchen. I sprayed the kitchen daily with insecticide before going to work and when I came home each evening. I swept up hundreds and hundreds of these little brown beetles.

I started looking for somewhere else to live. When my mother spent a weekend with me, she saw my spots and was horrified. She said they were caused by bedbugs. She recognised them from her childhood. I sprayed the bed with so much insecticide I was unable to sleep on it even if I'd been inclined to. I moved out that same day and went back home. I stayed there until I found a decent place to live even though it meant an hour and a half's journey to work every day.

☐ My immediate fear on becoming a single parent was that I would be a sitting target for burglars. News travels fast when death deprives a family of their breadwinner and protector and indeed there were a few rogues nearby who wouldn't have thought twice about shinning up a drainpipe. From the onset of my changed circumstances, I decided to sleep alone in my big, cold bed because I envisaged never having the nerve to sleep solo if I had one of the kids with me.

One day out shopping, I voiced my fears to my friend, Pete, and that evening he called at my home and handed me this ˙ object enclosed in a leather sheath. 'There,' he said, 'you can chop the buggers' heads off with this if they try to get into your bedroom.'

I pulled slowly and out slid this lethal looking short bayonet. The kids stood wide-eyed and wondering at the sight of me holding this knife but I began to feel a bit more confident at the thought of it, easy to hand under my bed during the dark, lonely hours of the night. The kids looked at me, puzzled, and I wondered if they thought their mother was going to suddenly run amok like some mad woman. I allayed their unspoken questions by making light of the situation and I secretly placed it out of their inquisitive gaze.

For years my trusty friend lay under my bed and I felt very safe in its company. Pete told me that the knife had seen service in Java and that it had come into his family via a relative who had fought in the second world war. It was quite eerie to think of the work it had done out there in the enemy-ridden jungles. Still, I didn't dwell too much on that aspect and I prayed I would never have to use it. Later, I acquired a sturdy black elephant, complete with ivory tusk and toenails, and he sat on guard duty on my dressing table, with his trunk facing the door, to drive out bad luck. I was thus ensured of double protection from my two talismans. From then on I slept soundly, knowing I had something to throw or grab if the worst came to the worst.

☐ My husband and I went to stay with some friends for the weekend and we were given the guest room to sleep in. It was a lovely bedroom with twin beds. As we hadn't slept in separate beds before, we decided to push the two beds together.

We got into bed the first night and were having a kiss and cuddle but just at the crucial moment, the beds slipped apart. We laughed so much, we had to hide our heads under the bedclothes so as not to wake our friends.

☐ I'd just been visiting a girlfriend. We spent most of the evening in her bedroom. When it was time for me to leave, I walked downstairs and, on my way out, I said to her father, 'Thanks for having me.'

'I didn't,' he replied.

☐ I share a house with two other girls. We each have our own room. One weekend my boyfriend, Toby, was coming to stay and for safe measure I decided to test the walls out for soundproofing. So I asked Raine if she and Brian had, you know, ever done it, with Claude in the room next door. Raine replied indeed she had and Claude had heard nothing. But Raine's mattress is on the floor and I have a double bed.

Only one thing remained, we would have to try out this bed. We asked Claude to turn her music off then Raine and I jumped up and down on my bed. However, she soon realised that a bed doesn't move up and down when you're bonking. It's more a forward and backward motion. So I leant against the foot of the bed and rocked backwards and forwards. This produced the desired movement and we realised that the headboard was going to present a problem as it knocked against the dividing wall between Claude and myself.

Laughing at the stupidity of this test, we asked Claude if she had heard anything. She replied, 'A certain kind of banging.'

☐ I've started using condoms a lot more since I came to work at the condom factory. At one time I was a bit embarrassed about them and I could never have gone into a chemist to buy any. Now if I'm in Boots I'll pick a packet up in front of other customers and read what's on the box. My bedroom is full of condoms; all my mates come round asking for free samples.

☐ The only mates I need in bed are fags, lighter and ashtray. I often wake up in the middle of the night and have one. I'm a bad sleeper. I think if you're careful it doesn't do you any harm.

Drunk or sober, go to-bed Tom,
Go to-bed Tom,
Go to-bed Tom,
Drunk or sober, go to-bed Tom.

☐ Our Vic and Charlie had to sleep together because they both peed the bed and me and our Reg slept together because we didn't.

☐ Both of us were out of work at the time but doing a bit on the side. All we had was my battered old single bed. One leg was broken and propped up on a pile of my books. I came in knackered after cutting an old scrap waggon up. Kitty had been cleaning up as the few possessions we had were scattered all over the place after a mega-drinking session. We'd been pissed for the past three days.

Kitty didn't start work at the night club until 11.30 pm. I showered, did not bother about pyjamas and slumped under the covers in the nude. There was just room for us to sleep side by side, Kitty being a well-built lass. I wasn't surprised to feel her slip in beside me. In the back of my mind I knew what she was really after. She could always turn me on no matter what state I was in.

In a few seconds the bed was heaving, the springs were creaking and then, with a final merry thrust at the moment of ultimate conclusion, disaster struck! The bed broke in half and the other three legs went through the floor. We ended up in a tangled heap and we needed a new bed.

Next morning I went to the 'pancrack' to fill in a loan grant form for a new bed.

☐ With nine people to look after, bedlinen was a constant headache for my mother. Eight sheets and pillowcases were washed, bleached, starched and ironed. To ensure that everybody's bed was clean Ma had worked out a rigid system which allowed her to change our bedlinen every fortnight.

As is inevitable with five children close together, there were epidemics of various childhood illnesses which resulted in greatly increased demand for clean sheets and caused a temporary breakdown in her system. For Ma, buying new bed linen was a serious and enjoyable enterprise. It started with a planning phase followed by market research. After weeks of scrimping and saving it culminated in a new quilt cover followed by the complementary pillowcases as soon as some more money was saved up.

☐ People aren't embarrassed any more and will make it plain when they are going out on a romantic weekend. They'll ask for four poster beds and sunken baths. You can usually obtain them but they cost extra. Any good five star hotel will have them. A normal weekend in Amsterdam costs in the region of 250 but you can add 50 for extras.

☐ Me and my new girlfriend went away for a weekend in Stratford. We spent all the afternoon in bed but didn't make too much noise.

That evening, in conversation with the landlady, she told us how some couples came to her house for sex. What she said was always distanced but I knew that it was us she was talking about.

☐ I love having a sleep with my boyfriend in the afternoon and watching him wake up, with sleep marks on his face, scratching his head.

☐ Earlier this year, on a day when I had nothing to do, I went to see my boyfriend in his bedsit. We went out shopping. It poured with rain and we got absolutely drenched. We ran back to his room and sat in bed, cuddling, watching the rain on the window and eating hot French bread and vegetable soup.

☐ When John split up with Carol everybody thought that he had got all he deserved. He was an adulterer twenty times over, witty but shallow. Other women who had been with him commented that he was hardly a sexual athlete. He had a big beer belly and was hairy but not hairy all over, just little tufts of hair.

'Why did you stay with him so long if he was such a bastard?' I asked.

'Oh, that's easy. It's never the sex with me. It's the cuddling. Ask any woman, that's what matters. I have never met anyone who was a better cuddler.'

The first time I slept on my own was when I got divorced. We slept two in a bed as children as there were seven of us. I got married when I was nineteen and then slept with my husband.

It's great sleeping alone. I can stretch out. I don't get lonely. It's a great feeling of freedom.

I won't let my husband get into bed with me during the summer. It's too hot and he sweats a lot. I love to stretch out and keep cool. I suppose he goes on to the sofa. I don't really know and I don't care either.

Ours is a secondhand bed. It's from my husband's first marriage and it's seen plenty of other occupants in between.

When I go to bed I go to bed to sleep. I'd actually prefer single beds but my husband works nights so during the week that's okay. It's at the weekends it becomes a problem. I go to bed first − I like to relax with a glass of wine and perhaps a video. When I hear him locking up, the sounds of him putting coal on the fire, letting the dog out, coming up the stairs and switching on the light, I pretend to be asleep.

I like to sleep in the middle of the bed but at weekends I have to make a choice. I usually go for the wall side. During the week I move to the other side ready to get up for work after he comes in at 6.30 in the morning.

I associate being in bed as being comfortable while snuggling into a continental quilt. Not so Hannah, who's three. When she climbs into our bed at four in the morning, she'll settle herself under the cover but after a few minutes, she pushes it away or crawls on top of it. I wonder if that goes back to her very first bed which was a plastic covered surface under a heat lamp in a special care baby unit where she spent her first few days. She did not wear anything but the heat lamp kept her comfortable.

When we were kids, we were always bathed and in bed by seven o'clock. Ours was a big iron bedstead with a flock mattress. I was made to sleep at the bottom of the bed and my two sisters at the top. If it was cold I used to cry so they would let me sleep at the top with them. We used to play telephones by taking the brass knobs off the bed. I liked to listen to my sisters' stories in bed but was always threatened, 'If you tell me mam, I'll kill you.'

One night I could hear scratching under the bed and thought we had mice.

'Oh go to sleep, you're imagining things,' my sister said.

After some time I realised it was her, scraping her fingernails on the iron bedstead.

My sister and I were sharing bunk beds on holiday. We were both very drunk and I turned the light on when she was trying to get to sleep so she punched me twice. She put an old squashed banana in my bed and I was reported to the Hotel Manager for being sick in my bed. She was 21 then.

I used to love to sleep with my granny. She lived in a back-to-back house which was very tiny. One room downstairs and two bedrooms up. The small bedroom would hold a single bed and nothing else, not even a chair. The big bedroom had my granny's double bed, wardrobe, drawers and washstand. I'll never forget that smell of Granny's room, not really offensive, but they didn't wash their linen as often in those days. I wish I had some of the things that she had in her bedroom. They were probably thrown out when she died.

'That's enough,' I said severely to my dog, 'I can't sleep with you making that racket.' I kept saying it.

She was usually very good, sleeping nightly on the end of my bed, although taking up a large amount of room for a Cairn terrier. It's funny how large an animal becomes when competing for bed space, lying plonk in the middle, nose to tail. My legs were threaded down a narrow channel each side. It's a wonder I didn't grow up distorted and bow-legged, moulded round a dog.

Once or twice I jerked my foot, not exactly to kick her into silence but to remind her that I was still there. It was school in the morning and I would welcome some peace.

'Just shut up!' I said ten minutes later. 'All that snuffling and licking, it's irritating. And keep still.'

Half an hour later I was near to tears. 'I'm fed up with you,' I said and kicked hard under the bedclothes, my patience at an end. 'That's the last time you sleep here. Off!'

There was a movement, a pause and a thud as she jumped to the floor and although the scuffling continued it was less annoying and I fell asleep.

I woke in the morning to find she had produced two puppies under the bed and I apologised profusely. She didn't seem to hold a grudge at all, but smiled, ears back, understanding. We were good friends really.

When I told them at school that my dog had had puppies in my bedroom, they said, 'Eugh!'

I think they were just jealous.

☐ When my mother was a child, she had a ginger tom called, you've guessed, Ginger. One day she took him up to the bedroom and threw him out of the window to see if he would land on his feet. He did!

In the evenings my mother tormented a woman called Katie who walked past her bedroom window. She'd throw glasses of water on her and sing,

'K-K-K Katie swallowed a tatie,
Now she's trying to swallow the knob of the kitchen door
When the M-Moon shines over the cowshed,
I'll be waiting at the K-K-K kitchen door.'

☐ I was an only child and spending time at Grandma's made bedtime a great pleasure. Grandma and Grandad had a spare bed but I preferred sleeping between them because it seemed then that I was the most important thing. I didn't go to sleep until I heard my Grandad say, 'Is the baby asleep?'

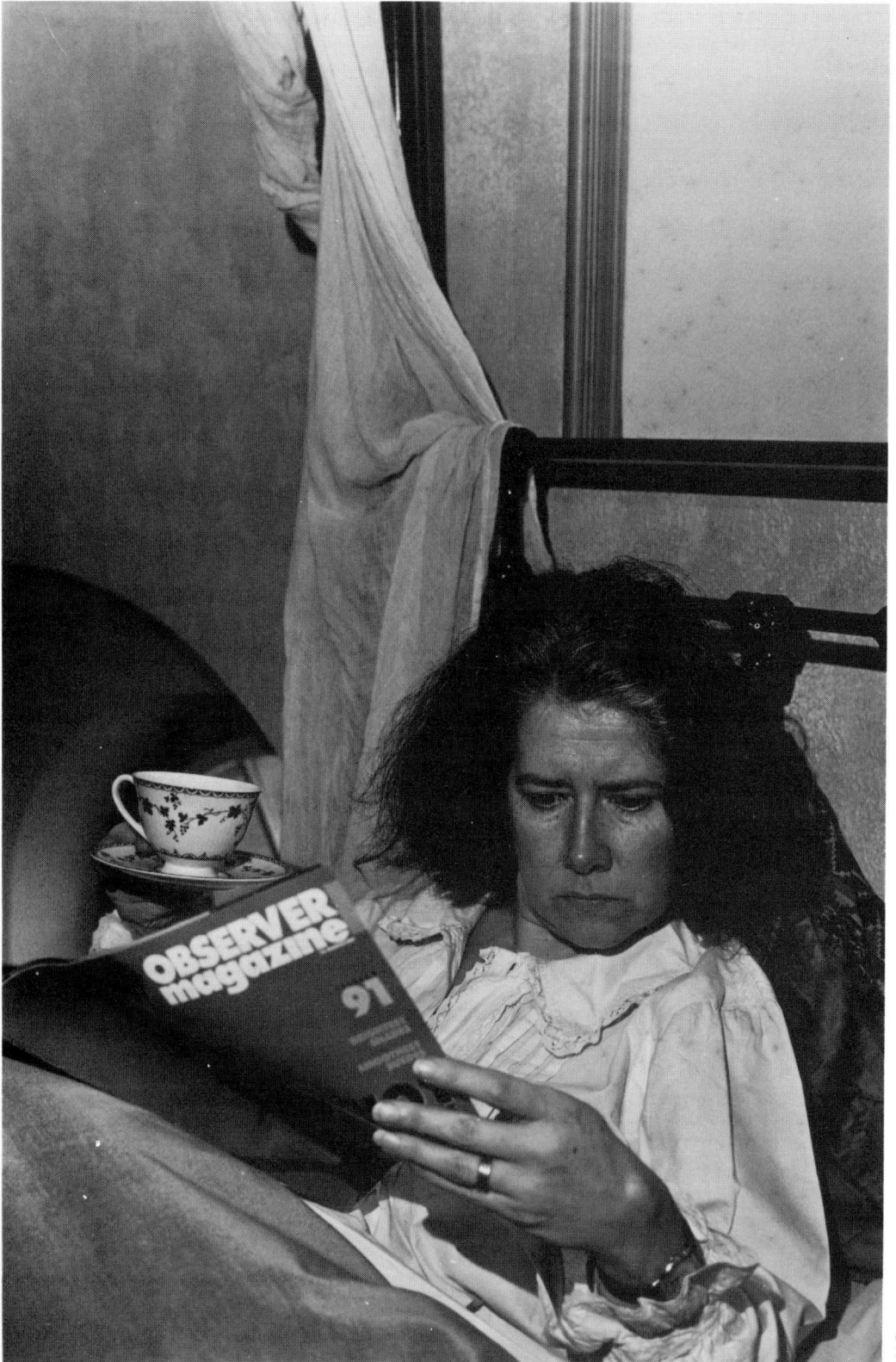

RITUALS

Here comes a candle to light you to bed,
Here comes a chopper to chop off your head.

☐ Why is it that bedrooms were always too dark, no matter how long Mum said I could have the light on? Shadows cast peculiar figures onto walls, crept round bed ends, made dressing gowns on the hook instantly into a companion for the whole night. No matter how many times I blinked, I could see his hood over his face. I couldn't see his face but I knew it was there, hanging effortlessly on the door. The pictures on the rose curtains were roses too — I know, I know, I've seen them in the daytime. I like the daytime. By 9 pm they are faced and bodied, friends of the man hanging on the door.

And that trapdoor under the bed. I've checked. It's gone in the day. It's there now. I know. I can feel it opening as soon as I walk into the room in my pyjamas. Someone's hand, no, no-one's hand, there's nothing, but a hand on the end of an arm will be there again to slowly push its way up through the gap — which is always under my bed even if we do a change round. I stand well back, I flick the blankets and sheet back with my outstretched arm to make my hole to jump into, my safety hole. And I leap longer than I can ever do in the daytime on Sports Day, it's not fair. But the ankle grabber didn't get me. I beat it again and now I'm safe for the night. It can't reach round. It's only the length of that arm.

The faces stick their tongues out at me. They must be the ankle grabber's friends. As the room starts to change shape, the ceiling corners bend and dance in the shadows, the walls seem far away, so far away that I can't reach them in ten strides. But it doesn't matter now, the man on the hook can stay there till morning as well if he likes. Goodnight. Alright. I'll put the light out ... soon.

☐ When I was in my early teens, one of my nightly rituals, when my parents were out, was to listen to the radio on my own. I liked to listen to Valentine Dyall, the Man in Black. His half hour series of ghost and horror stories used to scare everyone in those days.

One night, I was all alone, listening to a story which was slowly building up to a terrifying climax. I was sure someone was upstairs, sure someone was in the kitchen and positive someone was peeping through the front room door. I daren't even get up to close the curtains. As the tale came to its climax, I looked up and there was a wizened, ghostly face at the window. I almost wet myself. As I stared at the white face, a finger appeared and beckoned to me. I was mesmerised. I slowly rose and walked to the door. I opened it slowly, expecting to be grabbed, when a voice rasped, 'It's only me, lad, I've come to pay my club money.'

☐ I am the youngest of five girls and it was a ritual every morning for us to turn the mattress, which was flock in those days. Each year, we would put a torch down on our Christmas list, hoping it would be one which could be changed to red and green lights so that we could read in bed.

☐ I had a dream I pulled my tongue off. I was just looking in the bathroom mirror and

I opened my mouth and pulled it off. It didn't hurt or bleed or anything, and in my dream all I could think was, 'Oh, now I'll have a lisp.'

☐   I did go through a phase of writing down my dreams. I read in a book that what you're supposed to do is put a pen and paper by the side of your bed. As soon as you wake up, you start writing, otherwise everything just vanishes. The writer of the book thought that everyone dreamed every night and everything tends to be forgotten very quickly once you are awake.

I thought that was quite an interesting idea so I tried it for about a fortnight and it was true. I used to write at least a page of A4 every morning, all this bizarre rubbish that I'd never have remembered if I hadn't written it down. I remember, for instance, dreaming about a huge inflatable animal called Dog the Dragon, bouncing down a road. In the end, I stopped doing it because I like the sensation of slowly coming to when I wake up and if you are going to write down your dreams then you have to start writing the instant you wake up and it's a bit disorientating.

☐   I can't tell you about my worst night's sleep, because I have a lot of worst nights. My husband wakes me up and he's convinced there are two old women talking in the bedroom.

'Did you hear them?' he asks. It's the same in every house we've ever been in, he's obsessed.

Now I lay me down to sleep,

I pray the Lord my soul to keep;

If I should die before I wake,

I pray the Lord my soul to take.

☐   When Mam and Dad went out for the night my mother would ask her younger sister to babysit for us. This auntie was not really religious but she would put the fear of God into us kids. When it was bedtime, she would make us say several prayers before we got into bed. She made sure our eyes were tightly closed and our heads were bowed and our hands were clasped in prayer. She would put her hands on our heads so that we 'Couldn't look up and offend God.' She would say as many prayers as she could remember and by the time she tucked us into bed, we were too scared to do anything but sleep.

☐   I know it's a filthy habit but I cannot resist a last cigarette before I go to sleep. I always keep an ashtray next to the bed and three cigarettes ready rolled in case I wake up during the night. Whether I need a cig or not is debatable but the ritual pleases me. I put my arm under the pillow, lay on my left side and blow the smoke down the gap between the mattress and the wall.

☐   I am not sure what I used to dream about as a very young child but nearly every morning when my mum came into my room, I would be holding onto a piece of wallpaper which I had peeled off the wall.

☐   I find it impossible to go to sleep unless I have a big soft cotton hanky underneath my pillow. This stems back to when I was a baby and I had a piece of blanket to suck on for comfort. When I was about three, the blanket was replaced by one of my Dad's hankies, which I would hold round my mouth to soothe myself to sleep.

The habit continued through childhood. Every Saturday night, after my bath, I would pad barefoot across the landing to my Mum and Dad's bedroom and go over to the wardrobe where my Dad kept his clothes. The wardrobe was always open and I would stretch up and feel for the pile of folded hankies. I didn't always take the top one but I would run my finger down for the one that felt the softest. Then I would run back to my bed happy.

One evening, when I was about twelve,

my Mum came into my room. I was sitting up in bed reading with a hanky close round my mouth. 'Haven't you grown out of that yet?' she teased.

The next time she saw me doing the same thing I was sixteen and this time she was quite annoyed. 'The only time you'll ever stop that is when you're in bed with a man and you'll be too embarrassed to let him see you.'

Ten years on, I now live with Jim but the habit has held fast. Occasionally the hanky ends up under his pillow. He fishes it out and throws it at me with a look of mock disgust. 'This is yours, keep it over on your side.'

There I met an old man,

Who would not say his prayers,

I took him by the left leg,

And threw him down the stairs.

☐ I was very religious as a child. In the bedroom I made myself an altar. I used a stool, a cloth, a candle, a cross and the Bible. Before I got into bed I knelt in front of it and said my prayers.

☐ My bedtime routine always included a prayer before Ma came in for a goodnight kiss. As I grew older and more aware and frightened of death and eternity, I felt that I had to include everybody I cared about in my prayers. Not to include them would have left them unprotected for the night and any calamity that might befall them would be my personal responsibility.

☐ An early memory of bedtime is going upstairs in the dark to our large bedroom which had two beds. One was a single iron bedstead which had a base of iron laths which clipped over little studs on the bed frame. This one my Grandma slept in. I had the other one, a large double bed with an iron head and foot and a base made of wire similar to wire crochet. Both were covered with a wool blanket. The thick feather bed was shaken every day and a dimple made in it to lie in. I was afraid every night because the room contained a glass dome with several stuffed birds inside and there were some memorial plates of Grandma's dead children and several portraits of dead ancestors. These were made more frightening by the flickering gas-lamp outside. I was always pleased to hear Grandma come upstairs, the sound of her quiet movements, the creaking of clothes being placed on a basket chair and the soft murmuring as she said her prayers. Only then did I feel safe and content and would drift off to sleep under the red paisley patchwork quilt.

☐ I loved performing in front of the older members of our family. My party piece was a dance that was a sort of amusing jump from one foot to another. I practised it for hours in my parents' bedroom in front of the dressing table mirror. When Grandad found out I was admiring myself, dancing with my Mother's dressing gown on, he said, 'It's about time I learned you to box.'

So he would crouch down on the rug and get me to punch him. I didn't dance much after that but I'm always amused these days when I see boxing on the television and the challengers are dancing in their dressing gowns before a fight.

Elsie Marley is grown so fine,

She won't get up to feed the swine,

But lies in bed till eight or nine,

Lazy Elsie Marley.

☐ Lying in bed one Saturday morning, just after moving into our home, I heard two neighbours across the road. The sort of women who must have worked in the mills years ago and gone deaf. They have very 'carrying voices.'

'Eee, dun't sun sparkle on t'windows over t'road!'

'Aye, kid. But wait while t'sun moves round a bit. Yer'll soon see t'muck up on 'em.'

I'd like to say I sprang from my sloth, dressed in a pinny and immediately cleaned my windows vigorously. I'd like to say that!

☐ We worked a month on days and a month on nights. When we were on nights, I'd always waken up at 12 o'clock lunchtime with my feet and legs frozen. I'd have to get up and rub them to get them warm, until I was that tired, I'd fall asleep again. Winter or summer was the same. My room would be in the sun all day but it was uncanny. It didn't matter how much sun came in, I'd still wake up at 12 o'clock with cold feet. It must have been because of the constant change of sleep patterns with nights and days.

☐ My husband worked shifts at the pit. When he was on nights, he would come home to bed as I was getting up.

'Love,' he would say, 'it's wonderful getting into bed when you get out. You've made the bed beautiful and warm.'

The kids loved it when he was on day shifts so that he could put them to bed. He always sang to them. It wasn't a lullaby but one of the songs they liked him to sing best was *Cool Clear Water*.

☐ When I was only little, I always had cold feet. I have memories of times when I would curl up and put my feet on my brother's stomach to warm them up. Though it was a long time ago, I can still remember it clearly and with great fondness as it made me feel so warm and happy.

☐ I was once woken up by Prince Charles. I'd been on nights and had got into bed about nine o'clock in the morning but was woken up after an hour because I heard

Pontefract and Castleford Express

noises in the street. Prince Charles had come to open our new library and all the school kids had come out to wave their flags and shout 'Hurrah!'

☐ Some women don't like their husbands working nights but I do. I can get spread out. It's like sleeping with a bloody bulldozer.

☐ One of our morning rituals was for Jack to come into our bed for a cuddle. When it became Jack and Julie, we found our double bed was too small for comfort, so we asked a friendly local joiner to build us a kingsize bed out of solid pine. When it was assembled in our bedroom, I didn't know whether to laugh or cry. Instead of just having a headboard and a footboard, it also had 'sideboards.' It looked like the OK Corral!

☐ We don't often get a good night's sleep. Our bedroom is like a train station with kids always in and out. They come in our room nearly every morning but we're always awake and ready. Last night it was terrible, we were kept awake by our new dog. We only brought it home yesterday. It was yapping and whining all night but it slept all through the next day.

☐ My mum used to read to my sister and me *The Far Away Tree*, in chapters every night. She'd sit on the patchwork blanket on my bed and her voice always made me feel warm and drowsy.

☐ A circus woman told me she won't stay in digs because of one occasion when she did. The landlady's husband had died and without telling anyone she hid him under the bed that the circus woman used. After hearing that story, I developed the habit of always looking under every bed.

☐ My bed always had to be made to perfection before I got into it, otherwise I could not get comfortable. My brother's bed, on the other hand, was a complete mess – a huge ball of jumbled up blankets. When it was bedtime he never made it, he just used

to crawl into this twisted heap of linen and disappear. This was a constant source of irritation to me as I could not understand how anyone could sleep like that. Even today if the bottom sheet is ruffled up I have to get out and straighten it otherwise I can't sleep.

Old Mother Slipper Slopper jumped out of bed,
And out of the window she popped her head;
Oh! John, John, John, the grey goose is gone,
And the fox is off to his den O!
Den O! Den O!

☐ When I went for my holiday to my auntie's in Durham, there was me, my sister and three cousins. We made secret plans for a midnight feast. We collected all the food and goodies and found a place to hide them in the bedroom. We couldn't wait for bedtime and Auntie was surprised that we wanted to go. When we thought everyone was asleep, we crept to our hidden food to find it all gone. My youngest cousin had been up earlier and eaten everything. She was the only one who was fast asleep.

☐ It was Christmas when our Ian and me got into mischief. We were about eight or nine years old at the time. Lying in bed about two in the morning, one of us had the idea to creep downstairs and help ourselves from the cake tin. We helped ourselves to big pieces of cake and small drinks of Q.C. sherry. We thought we'd done alright as we crept back into bed without getting caught.

We carried on every night with our little escapades until our Mam started to question Dad about the missing sherry. He denied it, of course, because for one thing, he didn't drink and even if he had have done, I can't imagine him drinking Q.C. sherry.

Next night we tried it again, laughing because our Mam never dreamt it was us. But to our surprise, just as we had a mouthful of cake, the stairs door opened. As quick as the cake came out of the tin, it went under the sofa. It was too late, she had caught us! We didn't get away with it, I can tell you!

☐ I quite liked being in bed poorly. You always got food brought up to you and you were pampered. One of the loveliest feelings I can imagine is climbing back into a bed freshly made by my mother. All the sheets cool, straight and tight again. And of course you got the special treats. A whole orange to yourself, one you didn't have to share with your sisters. I always liked to press the orange against my cheek to cool myself down.

☐ My brother married a woman from Aberdeen and our family travelled to Scotland for the wedding. Whilst my parents, my older sister and her family shared a caravan on a site in Aberdeen, I was able to stay at the home of my future sister-in-law, with her parents, her brother and two sisters.

The overriding memory I have of that occasion is of the matriarchal nature of the household regime. The mother would wake up in the morning, sit up in bed and issue orders from this command post until she rose much later. If no-one was actually in her bedroom ready to receive orders, the instruction would be shouted at the top of her voice, provoking immediate flurries of activity throughout the house. This daily ritual suggested a queen bee at the centre of a hive being attended by a staff of worker bees who scurried around the ground floor maisonette, squabbling amongst themselves but always obedient to the queen. Any insoluble argument was taken by the disputants into the throne room for impartial judgement by the queen.

It never occurred to me during my stay that she might be ill but, a year or so later, I was told that she had been taken into hospital. They cut her open to do an exploratory examination of her stomach and saw so much cancer that they just sewed her straight back up as there was nothing they could do. She was dead within 24 hours.

☐ At the hospital where I trained, the doctors had a 'hit list' pinned up in their quarters. As each new school of student nurses came out of Preliminary Training School, the doctors would each select the nurse they intended to relieve of her virginity.

It was about three o'clock one morning and I was walking through the hospital, making my way back to my own ward, when I was joined by one of the housemen who was going in the same direction. As we drew level with the operating theatre he grabbed me from behind, his arms pinning me to my sides and swung round, using his buttocks to push open the swing doors to the theatre.

I was laughing and struggling, thinking it was just another houseman's prank, although there were usually other people about when they did silly things. He was as strong as a horse but I was also strong and it was with great difficulty he lifted me bodily onto the operating table.

I still thought in my innocence that he was just fooling around. By this time sweat was pouring down his face. I noticed the sweat and saw the look in his eyes. There was no mistaking his intentions.

I ceased to be amused and I became fearful. My heart pounded as I struggled even harder to free myself. He had a hand up my dress as he pinned me down with the other. By this time, I was really panic stricken. This wasn't at all how I had imagined losing my virginity.

'I shall report you to the Matron if you don't stop,' I said in a shaky voice.

He stepped back, his efforts had failed. Sweat poured down his nose and his hair hung lank, sticking to his wet face. The threat of being reported to Matron had scared him.

The strange thing about the incident was that we remained good friends and I was not really afraid of him at the time. Perhaps I was innocent enough to believe that he would not really have done me any harm. Sweet innocence!

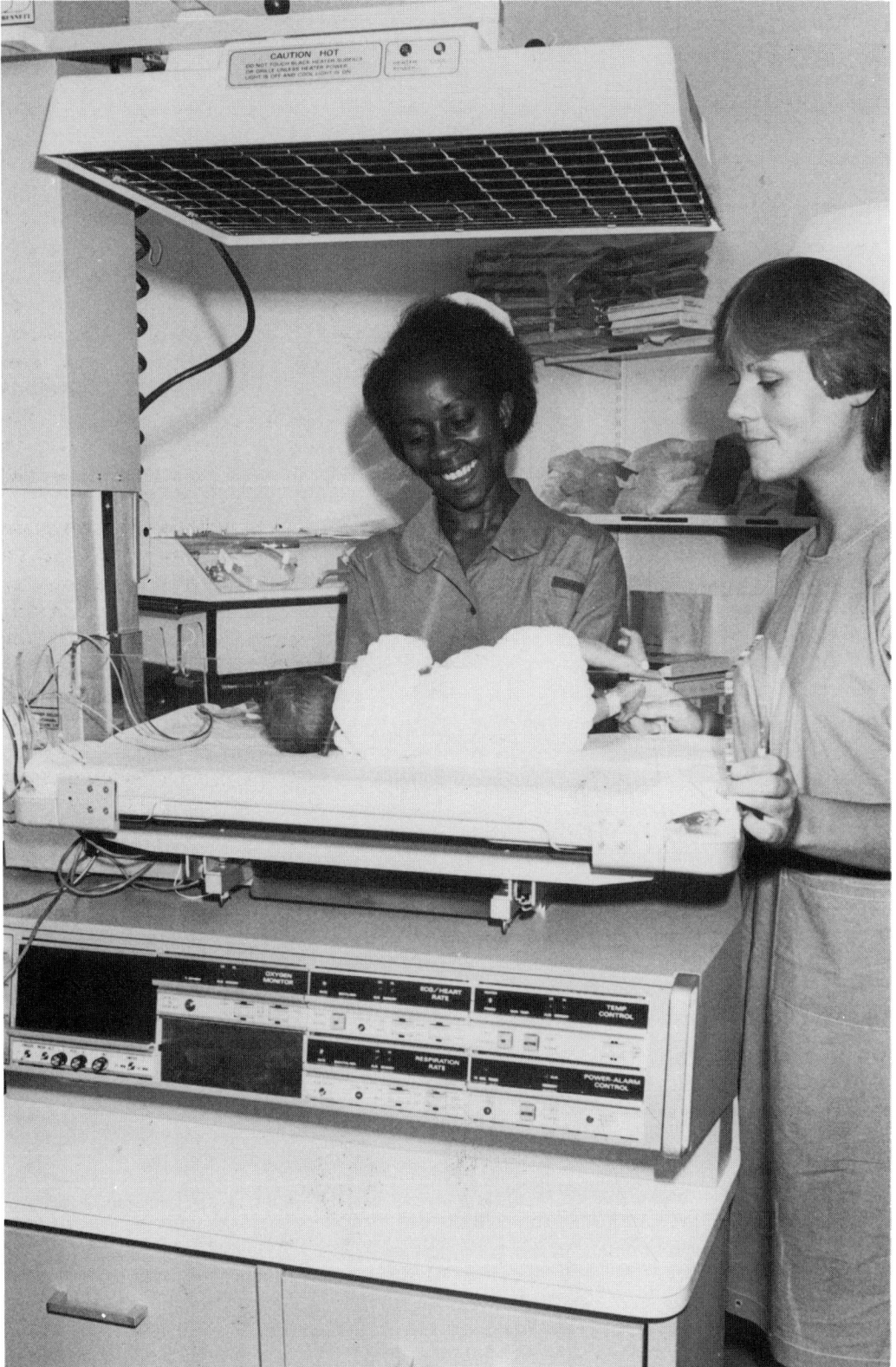

Up Jack got and home did trot
As fast as he could caper
He went to bed to mend his head
With vinegar and brown paper.

☐ The only time I ever contemplated suicide was once as I lay in bed. I was eighteen and feeling particularly depressed. I had fallen out with my family. I had no money and a gang of Hell's Angels were after doing me in. On top of all this I was suffering from chronic hay fever. 'I ought to end it all here and now,' I thought. But how to go about it? I could pull the pillows over my head to try and suffocate myself or charge headfirst against the bedroom wall or I could take an overdose. That was it! I reached for the jar of 50 hay fever tablets I'd fetched from the chemist only the day before then stopped. An overdose on hay fever tablets? A distinct lack of style.

☐ My dad brought the morning to our ears with his version of *Oh Danny Boy*, as he sang while shaving in the bathroom. When my dad was locked behind the door of the bathroom we children, by mutual understanding, knew this to be the right time to escape the unthinkable task of making our beds by sneaking downstairs before he had chance to spot us or our unmade beds. Once down the stairs, in the comfort of the gas fire and Captain Scarlet on the telly, we knew we were safe. It was fifteen minutes later. The Mysterons had just trapped Captain Scarlet in their secret underground headquarters and the gas fire was burning my legs raw

from sitting too near, too long, when we heard the word 'shit.' To my knowledge Captain Scarlet had never used the word 'shit' before so I assumed it didn't come from the TV. Then it came again and again, 'Shit, shit, shit, my back, oh God my back!' and then again louder, 'Me back, ooh! Somebody help!'

We made a dash up the stairs and my mam flew from her bedroom for us all to meet at the sight of my Dad, bent double over my bed, like a sour-faced chimpanzee, making funny grunting noises and pointing frantically at his back. My mam sent my brother next door to phone for the doctor and the rest of us helped my dad to lie on the floor, which was no easy task.

After the doctor had left, my mam told us Dad had slipped a disc in his back which would take a while to mend. I decided to go and see how he was as I felt a little guilty. As I neared the door of his bedroom, though, I noticed the door was missing and found this odd. Even stranger, lying just inside the door were two door handles and a screwdriver. My dad explained that the door had been removed to use as a bed-board and had been slipped between the mattress and the springs to give extra support to his back.

Bye, baby Bumpkin,
Where's Tony Lumpkin?
My lady's on her death-bed,
With eating half a pumpkin.

My sister, like a lot of nurses, is a hypochondriac. Ten years ago when she first arrived in Yorkshire, she developed a real passion for pork pies. In Lancashire where we were brought up, a good meat pie was as difficult a thing to find as a black-pea salesman would be in Yorkshire. Anyway, my sister would go through as many as four pork pies a day in an effort to compensate for her deprived childhood.

It was during her first term at 'Jimmy's' nursing school that she paid the price for her over-indulgence. She'd just snuggled down for the night in her room at the nurses' home, when she began to get stomach pains like she'd never had before. Her first cheerful thought was 'salmonella', so she banged like hell on the wall to her friend Sue in the next room. When Sue and a couple of others, whose sleep had been interrupted, arrived, they were confronted by my sister spectacularly writhing around her bed, moaning and clutching her guts. Sue dashed off to the main hospital building for a doctor. By that time the commotion was such that my sister's tiny room was filled with half a dozen or so concerned student nurses. After a few minutes, Sue arrived back with a good looking junior doctor. When finally he'd threaded his way through the throng, he lifted up her nightie and pressed firmly with both hands on the stomach area. Next thing my sister knows she's churning out the longest, loudest, smelliest fart she still swears she's ever done and half a dozen nurses are rolling about her room in hysterics.

☐ The funny thing about beds is that they never make themselves. If anyone ever invents a computerised bed, where you just throw a pile of blankets and sheets at it and then sit back and watch as it goes to work, they could make a few shilling.

☐ When Mel broke her leg we went to the hospital. She is a beautiful woman and it was a powerful image seeing her lying there, her face bruised black and blue, her eyebrow stitched and all because she had taken a corner too fast when rushing to a hair

appointment. Lying in bed pulled into place by traction she seemed especially fragile.

'Thanks for the grapes,' she said. 'Everyone brings them — and eats them. Eat away. But when you do, put the pips into the weight bag which is pulling on that ankle. I love the gentle pain which comes as the weight increases.'

☐ You moved beds as your state became less alarming. The first was at the top of the ward. I don't remember the bed so much as the trappings and the sensations. The drip in my arm made it impossible to turn over and impossible to get out of bed. There was acute discomfort through the night and then the embarrassment of having to pee into a bottle. Inhibitions go very deep. After a couple of days I was moved down the ward and then moved again further from the nursing desk which had kept me awake at night because of the light and chatter. There is one picture of my mother's face seeing an empty bed where I had been the previous day; the brief panic and the relief when she saw me, alive and, though not quite well, two beds down.

☐ In 1965 our decorator described his last job.
'There were nowt in the room but a bed with a dust sheet on it. I was stripping the ceiling when I suddenly realised there were a chap under the dust sheet. He'd been there since the First World War. Gassed. I had to decorate round him. Chain smoking he was. All I could see were the fag. Drove me mad it did.'

☐ Hospital beds conjure up for me good and bad visions. Firstly, on the bad side, my father died of cancer in a Gateforth hospital bed, my older step-brother Bryan died the same way though not in the same hospital and I had to suffer the unimaginable horror of watching my older half-brother dying of cancer, being cared for both at home and in hospital until his death.

On the other side of the coin was the good

which can come out of the bad. Watching my three year old daughter Georgina, waiting for her open heart operation, playing in the ward, looking so small beside what to her must have been gigantic beds. Then watching her being carried in the arms of an orderly, wrapped in a blanket, to the operating theatre. Watching the clock and the minutes ticking by, wondering how things were going and the utter relief at being told she had come off the by-pass machine and the operation was successful and she was now in intensive care. Walking through the door to the Intensive Care Unit was an experience I will never forget. I had been asked if I would like to go in with someone – my husband could not face going in until the second day – but I declined the offer. Had I known then what I was to witness, I would have said yes but my thoughts were only of seeing my daughter so I went through the sterilisation procedure and made my way in. The sight which met me was indescribable. Georgina lay there completely naked on an enormous sloping bed with draining tubes and monitor wires attached to various parts of her body. Had the Chaplain not been there I would have ended on the floor in a dead faint.

He caught my arm and sat me down. The next few days were spent in constant vigil until Georgina was allowed back onto Ward 7, carried in the arms of her very protective father to a bed, which was still too large, complete with sheets and colourful quilt.

Although the next seven weeks were to be the longest I have experienced, Georgina finally came home and I could at last tuck her up in her own bed. From that time on she was treated as a normal healthy child. She did not get unnecessarily breathless, her fingers and lips did not go blue and she could go to Nursery School, a promise which we and her surgeon had made before her operation and she had longed for for over twelve months. It is true good can come out of bad. I know.

Fever, fever, stay away,

Don't come in to my bed today.

☐ I had the misfortune of trapping a nerve in my back and I had to go on traction in a hospital bed. Talk about torture. I was laid flat and weights were attached to each of my legs to try to release the trapped nerve. When I needed toilet facilities a nurse would lift the weights up onto the bed and place in position the appropriate bed pan. That was two reliefs in one go. When I washed it was with a bowl nearby and, leaning up on my elbows, I would flannel and soap as best I could. My word, were my elbows sore. I had cream rubbed in by the staff and it was a welcome relief. It was just a case of 'like roses they grow on you.'

☐ When I was little and a bit poorly in bed, Dad used to bring things up to entertain me, a kitten or something like that. Once he brought in three goats and they jumped all over the bed.

☐ When I was about three years old my father took me to the Isle of Wight to see his brother. On our return the bus broke down and we were eight hours on the bus without a drink, causing me to become very ill and hallucinate. I remember being in bed watching monkeys playing on my mother's wicker washing basket which was fastened on the bedroom wall over my nightlight. I dare not go to sleep in case the monkeys came down onto the bed. During the next part of my illness, I remember being downstairs in the front room with heavy curtains closed against the daylight and a man standing next to my mother saying I had to stay in bed in that room for three weeks. That is all I remember; I do not even remember getting better.

☐ 'What is it, Paddy?'
'Will you marry me, Nurse?'
'Of course I will, Paddy, next week if you want.'
I was working as a ward orderly and Paddy, the poor old bugger, was on his last legs. I said I'd marry him to cheer him up. He looked that pitiful laying on his bed. Sister

Skinner came up to me later and said, 'You've done a right thing you have, promising to marry Paddy.'

'It was only a joke.'

'Well, he hasn't taken it as a joke. He's sent out for a new shirt and asked me to phone a priest.'

I was afraid to go back on the ward as I couldn't face him. All the others were coming up to me and saying, 'He means it, May, he means it, you know.'

Paddy died at three o'clock that morning. I think it's fair to say he went a happy man.

I collected enough for two wreaths. Sister Skinner said that it was the nicest thing that had been done at Hightown Hospital and she gave me permission to go down to collect them myself.

☐ A wise old crony told me that the reason why doctors and nurses are promiscuous is because they are constantly in the presence of beds. I would agree but add that since the great themes of existence, birth and death, 'whence came I and wither am I going,' are part of their everyday working life, they are forced to dwell on sex.

☐ Dr Sloan had a delightful bedside manner. He surely must have kissed the Blarney stone. He had the ability to arrive to see a patient, sit on the bed edge and hand out the most wonderful psychological poultice, encouraging you to 'Try to make an effort' for him and he would 'Come later in the day to see if you were feeling better.' He would come, drink tea, eat my mum's homemade cake, perhaps stay to tea and encourage the kids who were ill and not wanting to eat, to eat with him. You always did because you felt you could not let him down.

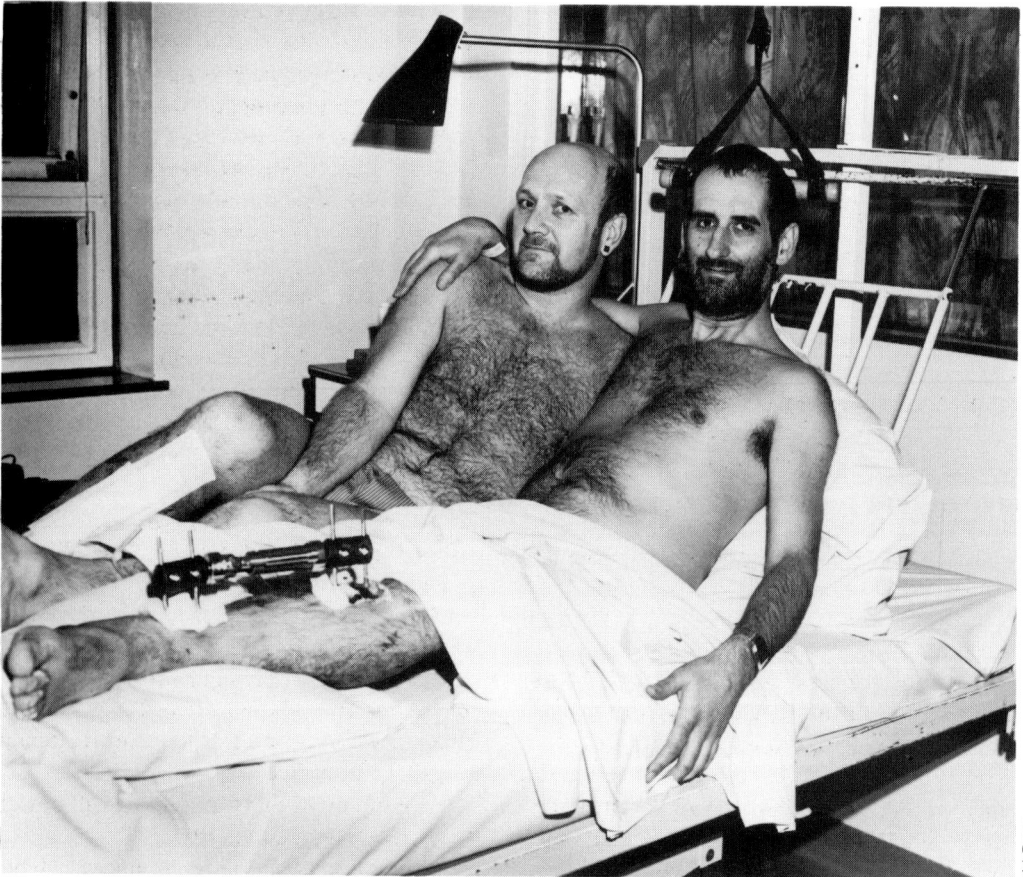

Val Green

42

☐ My dad was a stickler for dosing us as children. Winter mornings we had to queue up in the kitchen before going to school and take a large spoonful of malt and cod liver oil. 'Best thing out for keeping colds at bay,' he used to say. As he stuck the spoon into our open mouths we'd nip our noses. In the spring we were dosed with brimstone and treacle so that we didn't get heat bumps. 'Purifies the blood,' he told my mother.

One Friday night he insisted my brothers take a Beecham's pill. They refused to because they knew what the results would be.

'I'll not let them get the better of me.'

He stormed upstairs and stood over my brothers, pulled the sheets down from their buried heads, made them open their mouths, put a pill in, then closed their mouths and told them to swallow.

'That's the way to handle them. You shilly shally about too much with them,' he said to my mother.

Next morning when my mother went to make the bed she smiled to herself as she lifted the two pillows up to give them a shake. Underneath them were a couple of pink pills covered in lint.

☐ I learnt to play chess and draughts in bed. It was in a hospital ward and the lad in the next bed to me, Salim, was a champion. We put the board between the beds and he taught me till I became a fanatic. His family were millionaires in Dar-es-Salaam and he was the spitting image of Tutankhamun. After he'd taught me chess he also taught me to swear in Indian.

☐ We would begin with a trolley full of clean linen and a nylon bin for the soiled. 'Good morning, Margaret,' Sister would say, briskly half lifting her head from the bed despite protests. The bed was then stripped, the mattress turned, a rubber half-sheet put over the bottom sheet and the cotton drawsheet pulled and tucked so tightly that you could bounce a coin on it. Margaret, meanwhile, would sit staring at her feet, determined not to smile until she had eaten breakfast. Margaret was like that.

'And now for Celia.' Sister would stand with hands on hips, wondering how to tackle Celia. It usually took three nurses to hold her even though she had a pulley. Or should we roll her? Celia was having extensive plastic surgery on her leg. It was very tricky and delicate work. Celia solved the problem for herself. She heaved on the pulley and managed by sheer muscular power to hold herself quite still until we made the bed.

'Very good, Celia,' Sister said, 'but don't do that too often, will you?'

Celia smiled sweetly and shook her head obediently. I knew she would do as she liked because Celia was like that.

A frail wisp of a woman nudged me. 'I am just going to the bathroom, nurse, if you would like to do my bed.' She looked pleadingly. I bit my lip, glancing at Dora.

'I'll see what we can do,' I said, rolling my eyes towards Sister.

Dora knew what I meant. When Sister began the beds, which was only if we were short-staffed, she began at the top and worked systematically around the ward. No skipping and jumping, no darting across the ward because a bed was empty for the moment and therefore easier to do. Dora knew this but she also knew she could not stand to be in the vicinity while her bed was being made. Dora had an extremely bad skin condition and she shed skin during the night and during the day for that matter. But it was the clouds of dried skin dropping all over when the bed was disturbed that upset her. Once she had got over her initial dread, the rest of the day could be got through. I cleared my throat nervously.

'Sister, Dora's bed is empty.'

Sister gave me a sardonic glance. 'Why! so it is nurse, how clever of you to notice.'

'Well, I wondered if we could do Dora's next.'

Sister opened her mouth to cut me off at my knees. That's how Nursing Sisters were in those days. But she must have noticed some pleading in my face.

'Alright, nurse, just for you, we will deviate from the straight and narrow.'

Sister always became pompous when

trying to be witty. Dora, who had been standing by, waiting to see the outcome, sighed with relief and set off for the bathroom. Even Margaret smiled.

□   There was this chap in Northallerton Hospital. He'd gone in for an operation, something to do with his waterworks. The operation went alright. The trouble came afterwards. He fell out of bed and broke his hip. Still there I think. Came in with his prostate and ended up prostrate.

□   A few years ago a woman lived across the road from us who worked as a Sister at the local hospital. One day my mother, this woman and I were having a girly sort of chat about 'bedroom activities', which immediately sent our friend into gales of laughter.

'You would not believe some of the people we get in Casualty,' she explained.

Apparently, some years in the past, a very red faced young man entered the ward. He had taken to bed one day one of the oldfashioned poker stands that people used to keep by the fireplace, the ones with the poker, brush and coal tongs dangling from it and the round hole at the top so as you could pick the whole caboodle up. A companion set I think it was called. Anyway, as he got more and more fond of this handle, he got increasingly more aroused, eventually swelling up so much he couldn't remove the thing from his person. After much tugging he had to resort to the hospital to free him.

'You mean he had to walk into Casualty with the full poker stand dangling off him?' we asked, through tears of mirth.

'Oh, aye,' said our friend, 'but the best thing was he'd ridden his bike all the way there.'

Hush-a-bye, baby, on the tree top

When the wind blows, the cradle will rock:

When the bough breaks, the cradle will fall,

Down will come baby, cradle and all.

□   Mother always purchased a second-hand single bed for each birth and this was set up a few weeks before the delivery. Other items in the room were a bedside table and a chipped enamel bowl. The bed had a feather mattress. We loved to try it out, the crinkling sheets crisp against our skins. A large brown paper parcel was placed neatly under the bed. It was the confinement pack marked in bold red writing *Only To Opened by Doctor or Nurse.*

□   The sweat was reeling off. I'd been stuck in this bed for over twenty four hours and the damned pain was excruciating. God, they never said labour could last so bloody long or at least I never remember them saying so. None of them so-called classes could prepare you for this agony. Oh no, there it was again. I'd been having them for the last eight hours every three minutes and still no sign of the little beggar.

'Not long now, Mrs Stogden.'

'You've been telling me that for the last ten hours.' Stupid sod.

'Perhaps if you try walking around it would help you dilate a little.'

'If I could walk round, I wouldn't be laid on this bed.'

There didn't seem to be a part of me that wasn't in labour. I ached in places I didn't know even existed. There were places that didn't even belong to me. I hope to God they didn't think I was going to start eating a flaming dinner.

'Dinner, Mrs Stogden.' She left. Her head reappeared round the door.

'Perhaps your husband could eat the dinner if you're not very hungry, Mrs Stogden.'

She didn't know but the man with me was my brother. I didn't have a husband. She disappeared back into the corridor. My brother looked at the dinner, then at me.

'Can I have it then?'

'Well, I don't want it, do I?'

The last thing I wanted to face was a cooked dinner. I was cooked enough inside my head, letting myself in for all this. I just

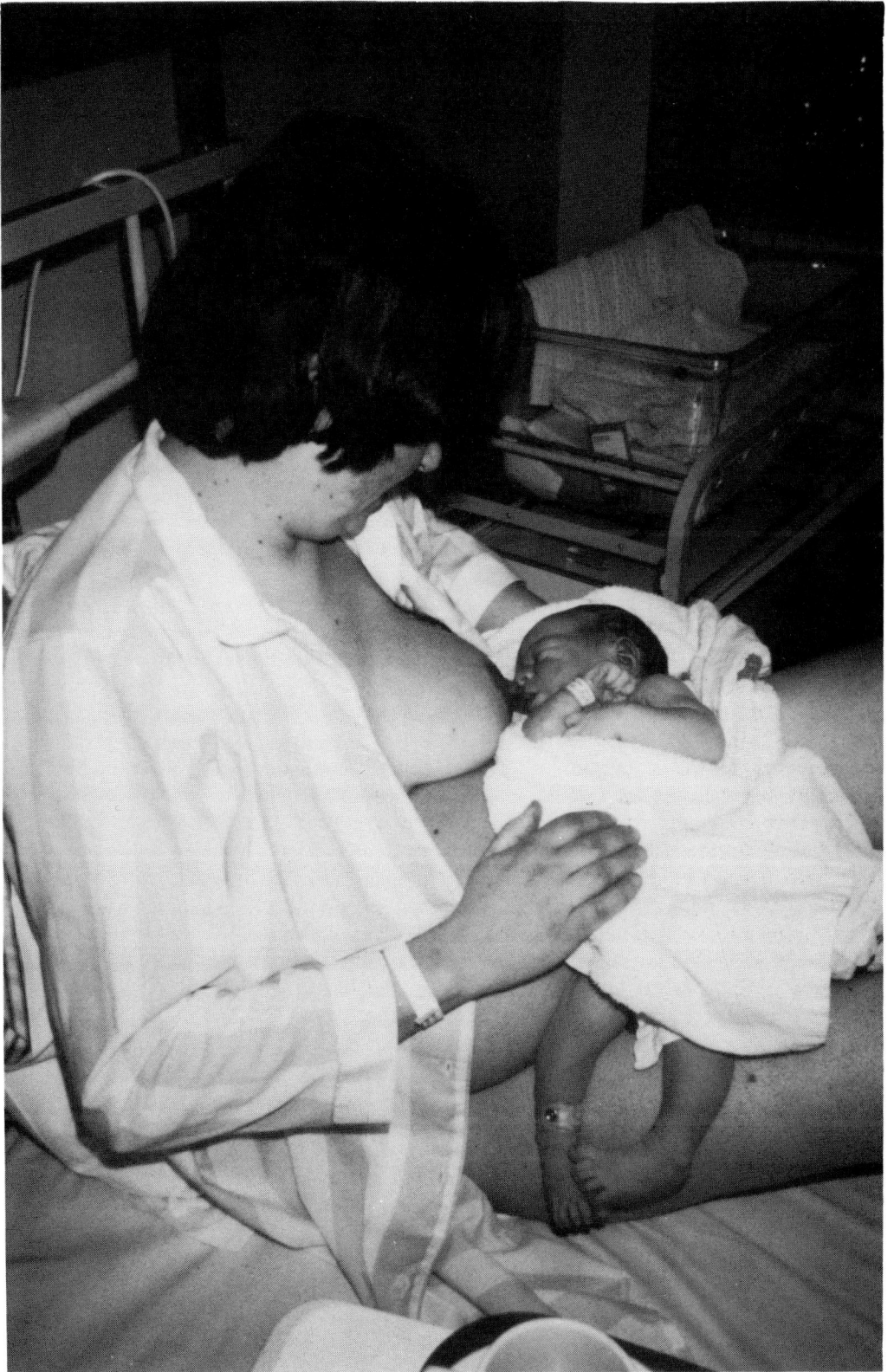

could not get comfortable, no easy position to ease myself into. A pity they couldn't mould beds for pregnant women.

I opened my eyes to find myself in what obviously must be the labour room.

'They've just fetched you in. You've been asleep over two hours.'

The pain was even worse and I sure didn't think that was possible. There was definitely going to be no break in the pains. My hair was stuck to my head and felt false. My mother was chatting away to the nurse. Looking around I could see two stirrups, God! how did they get my legs into them things without me waking up? The nurse smiled.

'You must have been dead beat when they transferred you through here.' Another smile. 'You won't be long now, just another half an hour, now you're ready to push.'

A head popped round the door, all teeth and no hair.

'Need any help Sister?' said Teeth.

'No thanks, nurse.' Thank God. 'Right, are you ready to push, Mrs Stogden?'

It was all I could do to nod my head in reply.

'You can start pushing whenever you're ready.'

Whenever I was ready? What sort of statement was that? As far as I was concerned, I'd been ready for the last six months. I'd had enough.

This was where it really started.

'Just pant now.'

I laughed. 'What, like a dog?'

The nurse smiled. 'I know it's a stupid expression,' she said. 'Right, one last push and I think that will be it.'

My mother was busy looking at the bottom end of my anatomy. The head had appeared once again round the door to quickly disappear.

'Right, one more push.' One more she'll get. Giving one almighty inhalation of gas that had been offered, I gave it all I'd got. At the sight of the head appearing my mother pronounced it was a boy. The nurse smiled and on the final result confirmed what my mother had said.

☐   When I was in the labour ward I was told to pull the string above my head if I was going into labour. I lay in bed frightened, felt another contraction coming so I pulled the string. It had a bell on the end, which I didn't know about, and I pulled half the ceiling down in my panic.

☐   I was a midwife in the early days of traffic wardens. Attending an emergency delivery, I parked on those new double yellow lines. In mid-delivery, a traffic warden knocked on the door.

'You can't park there,' he said.

'Don't be bloody stupid, man.' I snapped back. 'I'm in the middle of a delivery.'

He appeared to recognise the uniform I was wearing.

'Alright,' he said, 'I'll put it down as 'unloading only.'

☐   I have always given birth in my own bed in my own home. On the last occasion, I gave birth unexpectedly to twins. My first baby was born and I was pleased it was all over and she was attended to by the midwife. Then the midwife came to me and bent over saying, 'Mrs Sanderson, there is another one.'

I think it must have been such a shock I could not bring the baby myself. The doctor and the Flying Squad were sent for from the Halifax General Hospital. So my second daughter was dragged into the world in a bedroom filled with people. In the bedroom was the midwife, the doctor, the Flying Squad of two doctors and a nurse and the ambulance men who took me to hospital afterwards.

Both babies were fine and weighed 6lbs 3ozs each. Nobody knew there were two of them throughout the nine months.

☐   I knew you weren't allowed to put the baby on the bed but it was much easier to change a nappy on the bed than anywhere else. By the time you'd everything assembled — bowl of warm water, cotton wool balls, new nappy, dry nightgown — there was no room on the trolley thing with the fold-out shelf you were supposed to use.

I'd been put in a room on my own because Stephen had a rash. It was quite a big room and very cold after the tropical temperature of the post-natal ward. At first I liked the peace but then I began to feel very cut off. There was no-one in the room next door and we were right at the end of the corridor. No-one passed the door on the way to anywhere. It was a dead end. Hours went by without me seeing a soul.

I only put him on the bed for a moment. It seemed so handy while I got the things out of the cupboard. I moved quickly arranging everything I needed. I could hear footsteps distantly at the end of the corridor and felt faintly anxious. They wouldn't be coming this way. I moved faster. The footsteps got louder, heels tapping quickly on the tiled floor. I panicked completely — I was going to be caught. I grabbed the baby off the bed any old how, his head rolled back, his weight in the wrong place. I don't know which bit I grabbed him by. Everything about how to lift a baby went out of my head. All that mattered was that I wasn't caught out. I felt like a twelve year old not an adult.

Afterwards I couldn't believe how panicked I'd been, how institutionalised I'd become. I was very aware that they controlled the baby. I could discharge myself but I couldn't take the baby with me unless they gave permission. I must be the best girl in the school, do everything just right and give no bother. And that meant not putting the baby on the bed.

☐ When I was about five years old, I went to my auntie's wedding and fell out of the car. Fortunately, I only suffered from shock and two badly grazed knees. I had two very large bandages on my knees and was ordered to stay in bed by the doctor. My mother made up a bed in the front room, right under the window. All the neighbours could see me as they passed. They would all look in and give me a wave. I felt very important.

☐ Attitudes to bed wetting have changed drastically. Washing machines and cheap sheets make it less of a practical problem. It was different thirty years ago. I was five and my sister was three. Our parents had gone away and our housekeeper was in charge. My sister had wet the bed that night and I will always remember how the housekeeper, quite a friendly woman, draped the wet sheets over her head as a punishment. I felt outraged by the unfairness. I realised later that the housekeeper meant no harm. She'd just applied the prevailing ideas of how to toilet train a child! Child psychology had a long way to go.

☐ The comfort of being in my man's embrace, when the wind is howling and the drumming rain rattles the glass. There I am, safe and warm under the covers.

Those are my recent thoughts of bed but the memories that linger are of fear, loneliness and bewilderment, as I lay firstly as a young child, then as a teenager, confined to bed yet again with another bout of illness. I was trapped by my chronic asthma, imprisoned by sweaty sheets, sick themselves from constantly clothing me. How the days would drag. My mother would leave for work early in the morning after leaving food and drink by my bedside as the stairs were too much for my frail lungs and chest. There I would pass long hours, reading, listening to the radio and trying to doze whilst fighting for my breath, wheezing like a rusty concertina and continually coughing into yards of torn sheets which could be burnt.

The doctor visited often and administered numerous injections to bring welcome relief. He also left copious amounts of thick pink penicillin medicine, which was just about my only diet, together with inhalers, cough mixture and stewed tea from the flask. Sometimes a school friend would call and clue me in on what I was missing, the local gossip on who was making up and who was breaking up, who was the latest to lose their virginity and who was pregnant.

Occasionally, I would be lent a 'steamy' book — my first sojourn into the world of rude fiction. I went over and over the heady pages of lust, incredulous at the naughty goings on between the pages. I moved between child and adult in my sick bed, mentally if not physically.

I missed so much the real world going on outside my room, downstairs, the front door. The world in which I had no part for so many days, weeks, months at a time, when I was held captive by my bloody bed.

Matthew, Mark, Luke and John,

Bless the bed that I lie on.

Four corners to my bed,

Four angels round my head:

One to watch and one to pray

And two to bear my soul away.

☐   Our bed is no longer with us. We passed it on to a lecturer after Paul developed his bad back. The new owners have asked us to go and sleep in it whenever we feel we would like to. We never have.

☐   I loved my Granny very much and I went to see her often. She had a lovely big chair she used to sit in and many times I went to see her she was asleep in the chair.

'Want to go to bed to sleep, Gran?' I used to say to her.

'Folk die in bed, love,' she replied.

As Granny took ill, a bed was put in the front room for her. I would go down and sit on the bed and talk to her and brush her hair. One day I went down and was told Granny had died. I was taken in the front room to see her. It was the first time I had seen anyone who had died but to me it just looked as though my Granny had gone to sleep in bed.

☐   I'm an ambulance driver and, as you might imagine, we get called out to a lot of people in their beds. In Gateshead, we once went flying over in the ambulance after we got a call to say Albert was dead. An old lass was lying in her bed downstairs, half-starved to death.

'Albert's been dead for two days,' she croaked.

Albert turned out to be the budgie.

□ My grandad was a right hard bastard. Even on his death bed he wouldn't give in. He just lingered and lingered until he was a skeleton who couldn't feed himself. He had a bag attached for peeing into and that upset him. He was embarrassed even more when I tried to put spoonfuls of dayglo-pink blancmange into his mouth. He just clenched his teeth and remained defiant as though to say, 'You're not bloody feeding me.' On the night he died he touched my hand and shook his head. There he was on his death bed and for the first time in his life he did something gentle towards me.

□ My sister was very ill and the doctors told her that she had only a few weeks to live. She was very brave and it was her wish that she stayed at home instead of going into hospital. She didn't want to be in a bed so she had a bed made on her settee in the living room. It was only the day before she died that she had to give in and go to bed.

□ All the rooms were the same, little boxes with plastic built-in wardrobes, a single divan bed and a small set of drawers, to house each elderly person. I moved in and out of each room, emptying bins, polishing and cleaning sinks. It was my first day at the residential home and I was anxious not to miss out anyone's room. I entered a bedroom at the top of the house to find it inhabited by an old woman the colour of salad cream, propped up on the bed in crisp, white sheets. She startled me at first.
'Hello,' I said in the most confident voice I could muster. 'Are you alright?'
'No,' wailed the old woman, 'I'm going to die.'
I ran downstairs to tell the people in charge. It was a rude awakening that first day.

□ When my grandad died Gran decided that she wanted him buried from home. A bit unusual and oldfashioned I suppose, considering it was 1988. The Funeral Directors duly carried him in with Gran directing them. She decided to put him in the bedroom. It was early morning and a shaft of sunlight was coming through the bedroom curtains. Noticing this, Gran's plan was to place Grandad under the window with the sun falling on his face. The Funeral Directors carefully manoeuvred him over the bed. Then Gran led a procession of relatives and friends into the bedroom to view Grandad lying in state. 'Eeeh! he did look lovely,' she said later.

□ When my old dad was dying, he begged us not to send him into hospital. He was old fashioned like that, he thought all doctors were butchers, waiting to operate on you. He really knew he was dying and gradually took to a single bed in the front room. Eventually, he couldn't get out at all and was cared for by us and some wonderful Marie Curie nurses. He spent most of the time sleeping. I had been in hospital myself at the time so I was not able to help very much with lifting him around but the nurses could cope very well. He was surprisingly heavy. I called in to see him every day, sometimes just to sit there as he slept, and remember. Every night we would say the same thing to each other.
'I'll see you tomorrow, Dad.'
And he would say, 'Look after thissen, old lad.'
On the night he died, I had just left as usual when they shouted me back. I only lived a few doors away but as I went in he had just passed peacefully away and I saw and heard his last breath. I thought I would have been frightened, not having seen a dead body before, but I wasn't.
My mother hadn't realised how ill poor old Dad was and it hit her some time later. Funny though, she won't sleep anywhere but in that bed in the front room and she's convinced that Dad visits her. Who are we to tell her she's wrong?

□ Many years ago, as a child, our parents would take my brothers and me to visit my grandma in Newcastle. In those days of steam trains it was a wonderful adventure. My grandma lived with my father's sister and their family and when we stayed overnight, my brothers and I would sleep in my grandma's enormous wooden bed. I recall it more clearly than any other time of my childhood as every time I slept in that enormous bed I dreamt of an Indian Chief. He always looked the same, wearing a brightly coloured head dress of feathers and beads, red and white marks on his cheeks and chin and dark piercing eyes that looked directly at you although he never moved, smiled or spoke. I always knew that Newcastle Grandma and the big bed meant that no matter what, I would dream of the Indian Chief. My grandma died before I was old enough to know what such a loss really meant.

Some thirty-five years later, my father, aged seventy, was terminally ill and during his final days, my family and I visited him. Although he was fully aware of his own situation, I know that his family all showed a sort of cosy detached 'not really him — won't happen' attitude and secretly prayed that the event would be somehow as obscure as Gran's passing. During my very last visit, my father, from his bed asked for some tissues from the drawer beside his bed. As I opened the drawer, I saw a photograph, all in colour — my Indian Chief. I asked Dad who it was, why was it here? 'Son,' he said 'it was my mother's.' I never saw that photograph again. I could not find out where it went but I felt that the bed, the Indian Chief and the memories would remain to me just a part of life's events I would never understand.

Some time after my father's funeral, I met one of my father's brothers, who told me about the many years that Dad had been in the army, the events of his war, the many accolades he had received for the meritorious service years I knew nothing of. The conversation turned to Dad's large

family, the many brothers and sisters I hadn't really met. I was fascinated by the stories that Uncle Harry told. He would not freely discuss my gran but after a few pints, he told the short story that was the piece of the childhood jigsaw I longed to find. Gran was a spiritualist and had been known to cure ills by her faith and in order to contact 'the beyond' she would call on a wise man called 'Toomak' — an Indian Chief.

☐   We had just turned Mr Crane in his bed and he lay on his side peacefully. He was 96 years of age and, on his own admission, had had a good life.
'It's hot,' I commented.
'Not as hot as the desert,' he replied.
'What do you mean?' I asked.
'You know, with Lawrence.'
'Was he a friend of yours?'
'You know, they called him Lawrence of Arabia,'
'You knew him?'
'Yes, I was based in Cairo and supplied him with the explosives to blow up the Turkish railways. We used to meet at Beersheba.'
'What was he like?'
'Just a man, just a man.' Mr Crane turned over and closed his eyes.

☐   My mother worked at a hospital that had been a workhouse. A lot of old people went there to die. Many of them were incontinent. One day just before visiting time she discovered an old lady, naked, writhing on top of her bed. 'What are you doing love?' Mum asked.
'I'm playing with this chocolate.'
The old lady had shit herself. She was always doing it. I asked Mum how on earth she coped, having to clean that lot up every day.
'I suppose you get used to it,' she said.

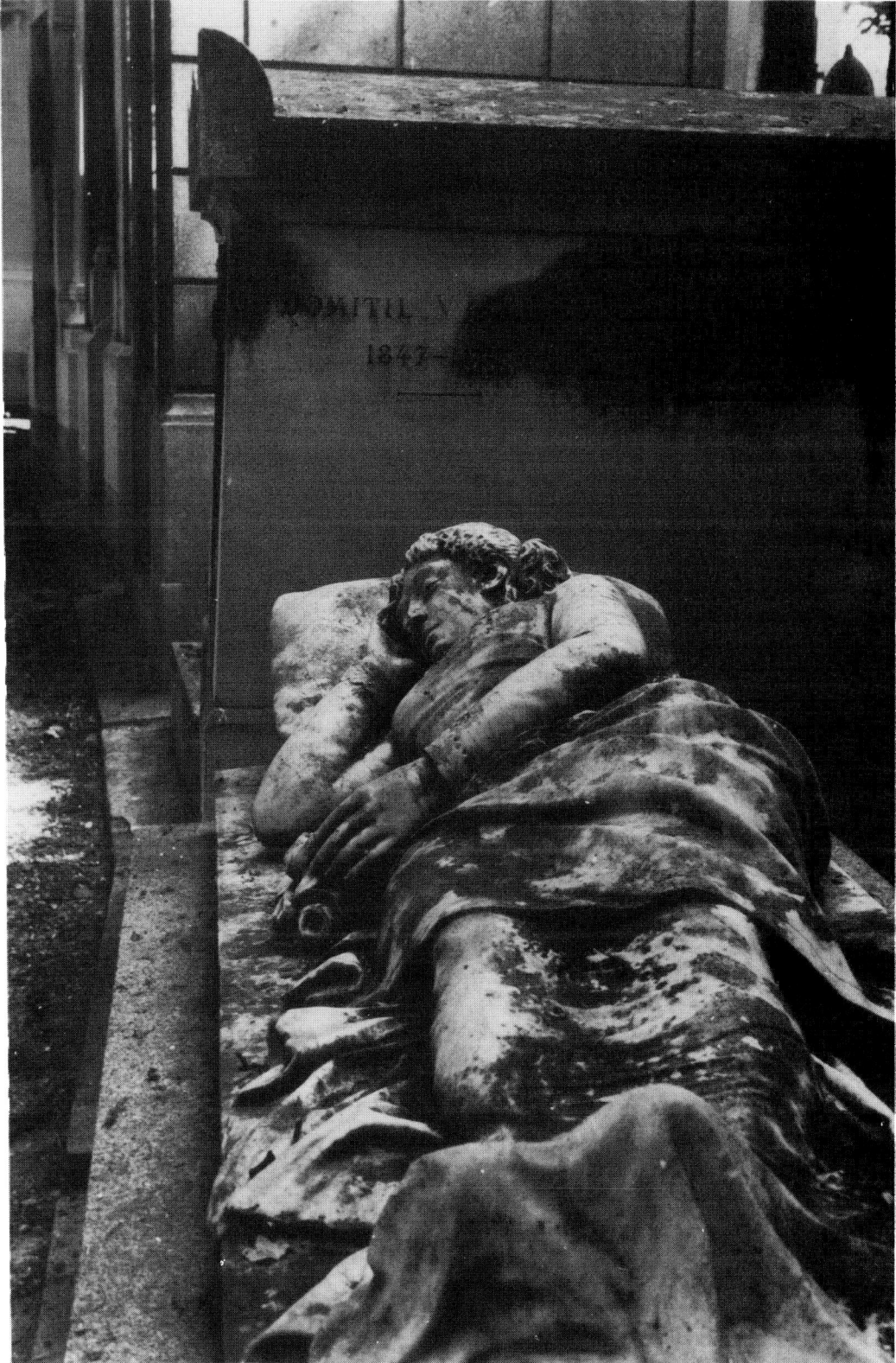

SLEEPING AROUND

Wee Willie Winkie runs through the town,

Upstairs and downstairs in his nightgown,

Rapping at the window, crying through the lock,

Are the children all in bed, for now it's eight

o'clock?

☐   A lot of funny folk work at hotels during the summer. Don't get me wrong, there's funny folk working everywhere but hotels seem to get more than their fair share. I worked at one in Devon for two seasons and had a great time but one night became a real nightmare after one of the wine waiters went crackers. I was laid in bed just drifting off when I heard this whoosh! and then I smelt smoke. I dashed out and saw the curtains in the corridor blazing and this wine waiter legging it. I put the curtains out with a washing-bowl full of water and then raced after him. By the time I got to his room he'd dived into bed and was reckoning to be asleep. I knew he'd done it, though, so I dragged him out of bed. Everybody came out when they heard all the shouting and commotion. It wasn't until one of the waitresses said, 'We've had our Guardian Angels with us tonight,' that I realised how serious it could have all been.

There were about twenty six of us crammed into an old building in tiny rooms. A fire would have swept through with no trouble. The wine waiter didn't seem to see the seriousness of it all. He denied it at first but then admitted he'd done it because he was mad with his girlfriend. I couldn't sleep when I went back to bed. I kept thinking about fires and choking. I'm always wary about anything like that now. I'm terrible for checking the ashtrays and pulling plugs out before I go to bed.

☐   When I worked by the seaside I had this recurring dream about the waves smashing through the bedroom windows and drowning me. I had that nightmare regularly. I've never had it since I came back to live inland.

☐   When you go abroad the first thing you do is run in the hotel room and bounce on the bed.
'What's bed like?'
'Urggh! It's horrendous.'
They're always rock hard. It's the nice thing about coming back home, getting in your own bed.

I've never been abroad and got a double bed; it's always twin beds. Our Laura goes in a camp bed at the side. We wait till she's asleep, then get in one bed to do what we want, then go back to separate beds to sleep. If you're crafty you make sure you get in the clean one and leave him the mucky one. Like at home, you always make sure you're on his side, then when you're finished, you've the nice side to sleep on.

☐   As a chambermaid you try not to notice stains on the sheets when you come to change the bed. It's a bit embarrassing. Once you get the hang of it you learn how to pull back the sheets with the blankets. The main worry is about touching people's possessions, sometimes you daren't touch them. I just dust round things on the dressing-table.

☐ I went to work in a hotel in Harrogate that was posher than the one I'm at now. You even had to fold the end of the toilet roll into a V shape. Most hotels use hospital corners, but the vallances have come in now with everything matching; curtains, wallpaper and bedspreads.

☐ Sometimes we break in on people while they are at it. We knock and there is no answer so we go in. All we can say is 'Whoops, sorry,' and go back out. That happens quite a lot.

☐ I've got a Z bed. You can't get them now. When my grandson comes he sleeps on it. It's really handy; it folds up with a table top.

☐ I've only once slept in a car. We were young and we'd no money. We were out for the day and we decided to stay overnight. It was on the A1033 round about Withernsea. Harry pulled up into a gateway off the road. All we had was a flask with a bit of coffee in it. The kids got their jamas on and their teddies out and settled down in the back. Harry and me pushed the front seats back as far as they'd go. I took my roll-on off so I'd be comfy. We'd just got laid down when 'Harry!' I shouted, 'the car's moving!'
We'd only knocked the handbrake off.

The kids thought it was a great adventure but I didn't sleep. In the small hours I thought, 'Well, we'll have that coffee' and I got up, heaved around and poured it out. It was stewed and horrible.

Next morning we went into Bridlington at 6.30 a.m. and had breakfast with all the fishermen at The Captain's Table. It wasn't until we were walking around mid-morning that I said to Harry, 'I'll have to put me girdle on somewhere.'

Now we've got grandchildren and it's got to the point we're pretty choosy where we stay overnight.

☐ We were doing the American Direct on the west face of The Dru near Chamonix. That's about 3000 feet of extreme climbing,

grade 6 in French terminology. You have to bivouac at the bottom of the mountain, set out at first light and then bivvy again half way up. That's the difference between climbing in the Alps and climbing in Britain. If you go out onto the rockface in the Alps you're committed to that mountain for two or three days.

We set off at dawn, about five o'clock, but had to slow up on the long traverse on to the face as there were some people two or three thousand feet above us, on their second day, scattering rocks off as they went up. It was really frightening as big rocks, I mean armchair size, came belting down and crashed a hundred feet to our right. They went at a hell of a speed; all you heard was a whine, then a bang and a smell of sulphur.

We made it to the bivouac ledge by 6 pm. It was about twelve inches deep and there are two positions about fifteen or twenty feet apart. We debated who would have which position, neither of them was very flat. We took off our gear and got some good belays sorted out. We'd no brewing gear but we ate a Mars bar each. I did doze fitfully but it was pretty cold and uncomfortable even with a sleeping bag and a bivvy bag. You'd slip down a bit and then hump yourself up again. If you weren't tied on and you rolled over in your sleep you'd have gone about 1500 feet, like off the Eiffel Tower.

In the morning we woke to good weather and a brilliant view down the valley. It is an unreal feeling. Here you are on this spot and you've got to perform really well to get back and you look down and there's Chamonix, it's so near, it's only just below you. There's a kind of wish fulfilment, you start wondering, 'what the hell am I doing here,' and thinking about just stepping off.

Above us was a ninety metre corner, overhanging steadily all the way up. If you open a book at 90 degrees, that's what it's like, completely overawing. The French term is diedre. We were shivering with tired hands and muscles but as the sun came up we thawed out. It's artificial climbing using pegs on the diedre and the second day's climbing is not so technically difficult and demanding as the first day's free climbing but this was where things started getting out of control. The Dru is a big and difficult mountain and on broken ground there's nothing definite to tie up to. We got up onto the shoulder to find everything coated in thin ice. We did three or four pitches of slow and dangerous ice-climbing and then we got into the mist.

It's strange how you do get used to a vertical environment when you climb. As you climb up the space grows with you and you get adjusted to all that space being there. The biggest worry is what happens if the weather turns. In an Alpine situation you don't have the time to complete a climb and get off the face before the weather closes in. You're constantly thinking, 'Am I going to go up or am I going to go down?' If the weather turns you have to abseil back down using your two ropes over and over again. If the rope jams you're stuck and your only chance is to be winched off by helicopter.

In the mist we never did distinguish the summit. There were several points where we might have been on it. The descent off The Dru is particularly difficult and we were lucky that I recognised the abseil peg with a bit of a tape on it where you have to turn right. We started down as it got dark. We'd go by the light of our torches; abseil down snowy ropes 150 foot at a time, locate the next piton, throw the rope down and disentangle it. I was abseiling down at about two in the morning and my torch had a dicky contact. I thought I'd got twenty foot to go when I was suddenly off the end of one of the ropes and the other one started pulling through. I fell about sixty feet in a complete somersault and then got my hands and arms on a snow ledge. After that we decided we had to stop. There was no level place to sit. Our second night we just perched and shivered on a 60 degree cliff till first light.

It was 2000 feet down the cliff and then a long jolting descent, three or four thousand feet, down the footpath. That's the point where your boots begin to bite on your feet. I remember the exact moment at which I realised I could put one foot in front of the other and not be in danger of killing myself for the first time in three days.

When we got down the valley Andy got on the train with all the gear but I kept walking to try and calm down. When we reached the tent we collapsed into it and lay there for two days recovering. I suppose it has made me think a bit differently about the idea of having to spend a night somewhere uncomfortable.

☐ I have slept on a park bench. I was in the Air Force and my boyfriend and I went to Brighton. It was real hot and we'd nowhere to stay so my boyfriend slept on one end of the bench and I slept on the other. Next morning we had to find somewhere to wash. We did this for two nights but we didn't sleep much. I kept falling asleep in the daytime. I was so brown from all that sun.

☐ When I first went in the Air Force, we slept on biscuits, well, that's what we called them. You shoved three of them together to make a bed. I suppose they had straw in them. You stacked the biscuits when you got up in the morning, then wrapped them round with a blanket to make it right nice and neat. The first night I spent on them I felt just like a corpse on a marble slab. You daren't turn over in case you fell out.

☐ I was in the navy during World War II and, returning from sea, we found all the billets full up. So we were housed on the HMS Victory, Nelson's ship, in Portsmouth dockyard. Hammocks were put up and some had to sleep on the decks. When the light went out cockroaches swarmed down the slings of the hammocks all over us and all over the decks.

☐ Possibly the seediest bedsit I have ever been in was in Manningham, Bradford. I'd gone there with a mate of mine to visit his University room-mate, who was now a young executive. I've never seen as filthy a place in my life. He had a two-bar electric fire for heating and a portable black and white television on a stool in the middle of the room. You could hardly see what was on it because the screen was grafted in grease and dust. There were newspapers all over the room, empty cat food tins scattered in every corner and a jumble of plates with half-eaten meals pushed under each shabby item of furniture. The bed was appalling, propped up on scores of dirty magazines. There appeared to be no natural top or bottom, just a big pudding of old and torn fabrics from curtains to settee covers but at least the sheets were clean.

We went to get drunk and later we had one of the best curries we've ever had. Back at the room Simon announced that Henry and me could sleep in his bed and he'd use the floor. I suppose we got the lesser of two evils. We all sat reading the letters page in *Men Only* into the early hours, with intermittent interruptions for loud trumps and raucous giggles as someone would read aloud a passage about a milkman getting it daily 'with a bored housewife.' I remember waking up about six o'clock to hear Simon on his way out to work.

'The shower's through that door,' he said, 'and the kitchen's next door. Make yourself a breakfast. See you again.'

I stumbled into the shower and placed a foot through the curtain. I pulled it back out horrorstricken. I had a foot like something from the black lagoon. The shower base was full of a grey, jelly-like scum. I was rinsing my foot with a leg cocked in the hand basin when Henry walked in.

'Don't go into the kitchen whatever you do,' he warned. 'It's like a pigsty.'

Funny thing was, when Simon went out to work, he'd gone in a beautiful three piece suit and a freshly ironed shirt, looking a million dollars.

☐   One of the funniest tales I know of happened forty or more years ago when me and some pals from Featherstone travelled to Lancashire to watch the Rovers play one of their away matches and decided to stop in

Groundwork Trust

Manchester for the evening. Everyone was warned the bus left at midnight, but there's always one, sorry no names, who misses the bus. Not having enough money for a hotel or a taxi home, he went to the Salvation Army Hostel, where he was charged five bob for his bed for the night. The next morning he was given back half-a-crown for not peeing the bed.

Now the day is over,

Night is drawing nigh.

Shadows of the evening,

Steal across the sky.

☐   During the war our area had a few air-raid warnings as the German planes turned towards Sheffield. When the siren went, my mother would shout me and my sister would take us downstairs. People seemed to have a second sense as to whether the warning was serious or not. If it was, then we all went into the shelter outside, but if they thought it was not serious, my Mother put me in the clothes cupboard at the side of the fireplace. It was lovely and warm amongst the newly washed sheets and blankets and my sister and me would sleep the night away in our little cubby hole. What an adventure, me on the bottom shelf and my sister on the top shelf. Mam and Dad spent the night drinking tea and listening for the planes flying overhead.

I often wonder today what might have happened if a bomb had hit our house. Would we have been safer in the cupboard? Obviously my Mother and Father thought so.

☐   I've slept in the Science Museum, Exhibition Road. When the doodle bugs were coming over we had to go down there every night. You got a rough blue blanket, no sheets. And I mean rough. If you got it on your face, goodness me, you knew about it.

☐   I was put to bed early so I was sound asleep when the air-raid sirens began to wail. My father woke me up from a deep slumber and wrapped me in blankets. I can remember thinking that this was an odd thing to do. Even odder was when he went outside with me cuddled up in his arms, followed closely by my mother and two elder brothers. We went to the next door neighbour's house, a lady who lived alone because her husband was at sea in the Merchant Navy. For safety we went into her cellar where I was placed on a stone slab which was raised above the ground by about four feet. I laid there snuggled down in the blankets wondering what the hell this was all about.

Knowing nothing about Nazi Germany or the fact that we were at war, I can remember thinking that everyone around me was behaving in a very strange manner. There we all were in next door's cold damp cellar, dimly lit by a few candles, for what reason I hadn't a clue. I must have got bored and fallen asleep because I cannot recall any more of the night's events. Next thing I knew it was morning.

With the return of daylight, my brothers took me to see the bomb damage and they tried to explain to me what it was all about. I was left with the vivid impression that somebody called Hitler had come over the previous night to try to kill me. Fortunately, he missed me by about 200 yards.

For years I thought that it was a personal thing between him and me. Even today, when an old film clip of Hitler is shown, I turn to my wife and say, 'He tried to do me in, you know.'

☐   I sleep in a guest-house. I've been on the council list for a flat but it's just wait, wait, wait. I work as a security guard on 12 hour shifts and you've got to be alert all the time. I get back from work at quarter to seven in the morning and the landlady's not up till half past eight. Then it's all noise, slamming doors, people working in the rooms. I've had 22 hours sleep since 27 September. It's February 28 today. I do four shifts on and four shifts off and when I'm off duty I have to leave the guest-house at 8.30 a.m. same as the others. It's a first class guest-house, cleaned every day, but it's no good for my sleep.

It costs £102 bed and breakfast and my wage is £92. The council pays. I keep telling them it'd be cheaper for them if I had a flat but nothing happens.

☐ We all like a treat. So when Alan suggested that we stop overnight at Los Reyes Catolicos in Spain, I jumped at the chance. The Hostal de los Reyes Catolicos is a sumptuous hotel and whilst one night may be a treat, more would be gross extravagance. We arrived from the airport in a taxi, passed the grandiose major domo who stood guard at the entrance and presented ourselves at the reception desk. Alan was given a card inscribed with the room number and a liveried porter gestured to us to follow him. The reception lounges were furnished with antiques and the whole place had the air of a luxurious museum.

The porter motioned us into a lift — despite its age the hotel was geared to modern living — and escorted us to our room. He turned the key and flung open the door to reveal a large, well-equipped living room. Crossing this room he opened another door. Ten beds would not have been cramped unless they were all as big as the one facing us, a half tester with drapes that would not have shamed the Cathedral altar next door. When I saw the bathroom — two of everything and all larger than life — I panicked. 'We can't pay for this!' I gasped, after the porter had gone. 'All our travellers' cheques will go on one night. Look!' I pointed to the tariff board on the door.

'Calm down, calm down,' said Alan, showing me the card with the room number and tariff. 'They're obviously fully booked and have had to put us in here rather than refuse custom.' The price on the card was more realistic than our surroundings so I breathed again.

'I bet this is where the Pope stays,' I said, flopping on to the elegant counterpane.

'I don't know about that but we'd best make the most of it, we're not likely to see this again!'

Pontefract and Castleford Express

☐ Everybody likes their bed made for them. But how many, during the 1939-45 War couldn't sleep because of the bedmakers?

It happened that way in miners' hostels. The snag was if you were on night shift, which I was for the first time. We came out of the mine at 6.20 am in the morning and headed straight back for breakfast. Then it was necessary to get your head down, and with the dormitory empty because the day shift workers had left, this should have been an easy matter.

In fact, it was the most difficult part of the day. After a couple of hours, an army of brawny women would come through the door and vigorously turn over all the beds, apart from the one you were sleeping in. If you stayed put, you couldn't sleep and neither could you get your bed made. The difficulty was that when the day shift came back at two o'clock in the afternoon, it was quite impossible to sleep through the din! So although the beds were comfortable, if austere, they certainly weren't made by Silentnight. It was next to impossible to get all the rest you seemed to need.

In the end, I slept in a manhole down the pit, after the deputy had been round to do his shot firing on the face and we had filled off. It is actually a crime to sleep down the pit but nobody was caught and the two hours on a sack in a manhole plus about four hours between clean sheets at the hostel kept me going for the week.

Tom Laughton, brother of Charles, the film star, was in charge of such hostels and he was very particular about his teams of women on the beds. He owned the Royal Hotel at Scarborough, where the beds were fit for a King and certainly suitable for Prime Ministers as was proved on numerous occasions.

Miss Lee ran the bed army and also saw that the sheets were virgin white. Tom Laughton praised her housekeeping to the skies and there I couldn't fault him. The last time I saw Miss Lee was at Butlin's holiday camp at Filey, when the war was over, meeting some of her former girls. She couldn't find anything wrong with the beds at Butlin's either, though they must be in a sorry state now, with the run down of chalets on the Yorkshire coast.

☐ Not many years ago, when I worked at the pit, 'beds' were a prime concern for some chaps. Early mornings and late nights made for many a tired miner on the day shift. The craftsmen had quite a bit of freedom inasmuch as if the job was running and they were not called for, a trip down a quiet roadway to find a bed was not unknown. A piece of conveyor belting was luxury but a pile of stones would do nicely.

☐ I left home because my father beat me and it was rows all the time. I'm on the YTS and I sleep in a guest-house. We have to go out at 8.30 in the morning and it's the same on Saturdays and Sundays. All you do is walk and walk. I walk from Shipley to Bradford to kill time. There's nowhere to go on Sundays – even the cafes are closed. I share a room and the room is fine but it's the rules and regulations. There's no visitors allowed. In the evening you can make a cup of tea and take it up to your room but you can't stay downstairs in the dining room. You can't go in other people's rooms either but we've bent that rule a bit.

☐ When my wife, Pam, was still my girlfriend, in those far-off days when we still held hands in the street, we decided to spend the Easter weekend in Amsterdam. Despite it being mid-April, the weather was like late June. The place was packed. Round and around the city we tramped looking for somewhere to spend the night; no joy anywhere.

We must have covered twenty miles, taking it in turns to lug the increasingly heavy holdall. As well as being tired in a healthy footsore way, we had a bit of unhealthy wear and tear on our nerves. Just by being itself, Amsterdam can do your head in. We had the extra thrill of a confrontation with a knife wielding maniac who wanted

Pam for his own reasons. I came within two inches of being stabbed that day and I was ready for a sleep.

It was just after seven with the sun going down when we found the Christian Youth Hostel. I've never been religious but when, after waiting half an hour, they told us we each had a bed, well, put it down to tiredness, trauma or both but I said a prayer of thanks. For the first time that day we were able to relax. We had a beautiful cheap meal and a couple of drinks but kept our eyes on the clock. Lights Out was at eleven, when all good Christians are tucked up in bed.

Before setting off for our respective dorms, we had a protracted kiss and cuddle so by the time I'd showered and brushed my teeth, the dormitory was in darkness.

My ticket number was bed seventeen. Eventually my eyes adjusted to the dark and I was able to locate my bed. I was so tired I could have slept on an ironing board but that bed was brilliant. A few blokes were chatting quietly in a language that sounded Scandinavian or something else designed to bring on sleep. I was as comfortable as anyone who has ever more than earned themselves a good sleep.

As usual before settling down for the night, I gave out a long, loud stiff fart and was rewarded for my efforts with quite a bit of laughter. It seemed to me that a bit of well-timed flatulence was just the thing to break down cultural barriers. I was laughing like 'Muttley' under the sheets when a disembodied American voice said, 'Excuse me sir, you appear to have my bed.'

I lay very still hoping that he wasn't talking to me. No such luck.

'Excuse me,' he says again, this time following it up with a tug on my ankle.

'I'm sorry,' I said, 'but can't you sleep in the one I'm supposed to be in?'

'No, sir. My ticket clearly says bed eleven

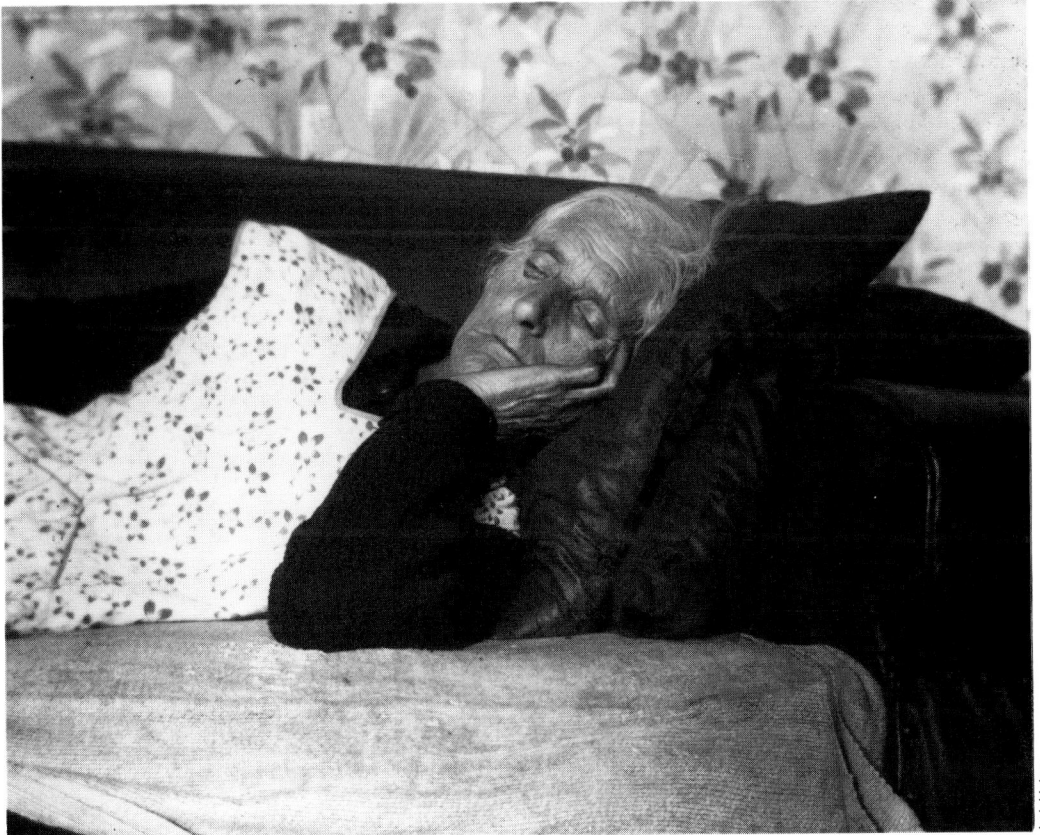

and that's this one.'

Realising that I wasn't going to get anywhere, I gathered up my sheets and belongings and went stumbling off in search of bed seventeen. Mind you, the smell I left wafting around that bed was more than revenge. To the accompaniment of what sounded like 'Thank God for that' in several languages, I settled down in my new bed. Twenty minutes later, according to my luminous watch, I was woken by a Spaniard; again I was in the wrong bed. This time there were more than a few grumbles in the dormitory, they were ready to lynch me. Quickly I showed him to the only other empty bed in the room, whispered sorry in as many languages as I knew and finally went to sleep. You should have seen some of the looks I got in the morning.

☐   My daughter and I loved sleeping at airports. When she was in her early teens we started going on cheap skiing holidays with flights which left at dawn. We've slept at Heathrow, Gatwick and Manchester. Manchester was our favourite. We'd go to the bit with big brown armchairs where the sparrows got in and flew about up in the ceiling. There were lots of Arcade games to play and that was special because they weren't all over the place then. The green metal chairs had a television on one arm and you could put a coin in to watch. Mostly we preferred watching the other people walking up and down, all on their way to somewhere else. And then we'd have a big breakfast early in the morning.

I once set aside a weekend to do something special with my daughter and she chose to go to Manchester and sleep in the airport. We hadn't a flight to catch; it was a treat just to soak up the atmosphere.

☐   I'll never forget waking up in a couchet to the smell and rhythm of the coal burning engine winding its way through the African countryside. We were heading for Victoria Falls and the sun was just showing itself from the vast plains. Me and my man, squeezed together in the lower bunk, hot already, half covered in a Zimbabwean Railways sheet. A sharp tap on the door, we unlocked it and a large sweaty porter is waiting with cups of tea. 'Good morning Sir. Good morning Madam.' We take our tea, with thanks, the saucers covered in a black film of smut. Zebra, buffalo and antelope can be seen from the window. The playing of an Imbira, an African hand piano, comes from the next compartment. Happy cries of 'Good morning Sister' are heard from the corridor. We glide into the station, a small settlement miles from anywhere. A mud hut village, the central fire glowing still and barefoot Africans board and alight from the train. All this and tea in bed!

☐   I slept in the Nubian Desert beneath the stars at the side of some railway lines. I was woken up by bright lights and horns were blaring. It was like a host of angels. I wondered where the hell I was. Then I realised it was a train passing by.

☐   When we arrived in Karachi we were greeted by hundreds of begging faces pressed up against the glass of the airport doors; taxi drivers, people with leprosy and queues of buses. We got on to our bus and were taken to the 'Hostelerie de France'. Why a small hotel on the outskirts of Karachi airport should be called that, I don't know.

Most of the furniture in the place was covered from head to foot in white dust sheets. It was as though it only opened when a bus rolled up from the airport. What with the heat and the dust and the tiring flight all we really wanted to do was take a quick shower and roll into bed. Heather went to the shower first and ran out screaming because men were peering with grinning faces over the shower wall. I then went to shower and ran out screaming for the same reason.

We flopped into bed and drifted off. Next morning, as Heather reared up, I noticed blood all over the sheet under her back and on the pillow. I shouted, 'There's blood all over, lass.'

Stephen McClarence

On inspecting her shoulders and neck I found pinprick red dots on her, hundreds of them and one or two on my own arms and neck. 'Bed bugs! I said it was a muck hole.' I charged downstairs and demanded to see the Manageress. 'Do you know that our bedroom is full of bugs?' She didn't understand bugs so I ended up saying small animals.

'I can assure you, sir, there are no small animals in my rooms.'

So I said, 'Wait there, then, and I'll prove it to you.'

I ran back upstairs and fetched Heather down, lifted up the back of her shirt and explained to an audience steadily increasing in numbers. 'What about that then?'

In a Muslim country where women are clad in baggy robes from head to foot, I don't know what they made of seeing a fully exposed and red spotted back. The Manageress just tutted and assured me, 'I can only repeat, sir, there are no small animals in my beds.'

I gave up and went to breakfast to find that half of the Malaysian National Soccer team, three Iranian refugees and a dustbin man and his mate from Bristol had also been bitten by 'small animals.'

☐   We went to Majorca for a week and found ourselves in a room next to a couple who were active to say the least. We would get in from a disco late at night and we could hear them going at it. Bang, bang, bang. Next morning at coffee we were naturally intrigued to see who the couple were. When they came out we were amazed. Neither of them was younger than 75!

☐   There was one man who had bed and breakfast with us from time to time. He was small and shabby, almost a tramp. Each time he had a different good looking woman with him.

'Can you show us a bedroom?'
'Last time you stayed in No. 3.'
'Could you show me a different one?'
I took him to see No. 4.
'Have you another?'
'Well, No. 5 is available.'

He looked in and was satisfied. 'Just right.'

Over the next few hours different pieces of furniture were put out into the passage; the rubbish bin, mats, a small chest of drawers. Next morning it was clear that only one side of the double bed had been slept in. He should have asked for 'Floor and Breakfast.'

Little Boy Blue,
Come blow your horn,
The sheep's in the meadow
The cow's in the corn;
But where is the boy
Who looks after the sheep?
He's under the haycock,
Fast asleep.

☐   Me and three brothers all slept in the big attic at home. One brother always had his bed polarised, that is with his head to the north. Every morning, my mother would move his bed back but each night he would polarise his bed again. He is 85 now and lives in New Zealand. He still polarizes his bed. I wonder how he does it in New Zealand? They're upside down, aren't they?

☐   All the hitchhikers of the 'Travel Round Europe on £1 a day type' never make reference to beds experienced. Not real beds anyway.

Cross-channel ferries have couchettes, which are dentists' chairs without the reclining function and minty mouthwash but with all of the pain. Overnight sleepers are encouraged to pay 'just that little bit extra' for an unholy manger in lieu of a crib.

But abroad and inland, the budget sleeper has often to make do and mend with only what mother nature provides. A bridge just outside Zurich was my favourite one year. It was next to the Lindt chocolate factory and I dreamed sublime Roald Dahl dreams in between times. Next night my bed was in a rainstorm. The ground was out, no tent; so a tree with extra branches. Heaven, or a little nearer it.

☐ In 1956 I was convinced that I would be killed in Suez so I set off hitchhiking to Edinburgh to see my girlfriend. The first night I slept in a dossers' guest house somewhere at the back of Morpeth and the next in a Salvation Army hostel just off Princes Street. There it was bunk beds. An old veteran with a wooden leg slept next to me and over the top was a heavyweight from the Sutherland Highlanders. The kilt was draped across the bed head. He told me, I remember, that certain prostitutes in the street opposite had their teeth removed so that they could gam better.

That afternoon I called up to see my girlfriend in her room in Buchanan Hall. She sat on the bed and I on the chair. The door had to be open – in some hostels they had to push the bed into the corridor if men or youths visited – but here they were more sedate. We drank tea and stole a kiss behind the open door.

☐ Every fortnight we go away to camp. About 16 of us sleep in the billet. We never actually sleep; we stay awake all night and have fun. If any lad does fall asleep, we pick him up in his sleeping bag and put him outside the door.

We have pillow fights. There's feathers all over the place and it takes us hours and hours to clean it all up afterwards but it's worth it. If we are in a barracks we have to keep the noise down as there is always an officer checking up on us.

☐ I was staying in a hostel in San Francisco, which as we all know is prone to large scale earthquakes, when the bunk bed moved. Then, just as I looked to the bed above me, it moved again. 'Aye, aye, what's going on up there?' I said to myself. This happened another three times during the night, which annoyed me enough to tell the person above to stop messing about. When I woke the next morning, there was no-one in

my room at all and there had not been all night. The earth moved though!

☐ I can't count the number of different beds I must have slept in. Before I finally settled down, I travelled almost ten years with showbusiness. Some of the digs were like home from home, clean and comfortable, but there were many that were not. One was very uncomfortable. The springs in the mattress were broken and they made a terrible noise whenever I turned over. I was very embarrassed by this, knowing the landlady slept in the next room. My husband thought it was funny and he would fool around making the bed squeak. Another bed we slept in was very damp and I caught a bad cold through it. We also shared a converted bus. The bed we slept in was two foot wide. If I'd fallen out I would have been sharing a bed with a young Indian man.

☐ We paid homage to Shakespeare at Stratford, visited the Vale of Evesham and Warwick, then continued down the Fosseway to Moreton-in-the-Marsh. We had been recommended a bed and breakfast place in a hamlet nearby. I can't remember the name now, perhaps it was Leamington. We got there by traversing the side of a field and crossing two cattle-grids.

The old farmhouse stood a little distance away and immediately behind the farmhouse was a miniature church and graveyard. From the landing window you looked down onto the graveyard, most of which bore the same family name.

All the windows were the oldfashioned mullion type with a few trees close by obscuring some of the house. On first approaching it everything was deathly quiet. No-one appeared to be about. After a couple of 'Hellos' we did hear a feeble voice down a passage. In a room we found an old lady in bed, possibly 80 years old to look at her. Apparently, a day or so earlier she had broken her leg. Her daughter was coming from her farm, five miles away, to cook us some dinner. She explained where our rooms were. Ascending the large stairway in dismal light and creepy shadows to our bedroom, there before us was an antique four-poster bed!

We had dinner and at 7.30 pm, we wondered what could we do until bedtime. Off we went to Moreton-in-the-Marsh for a stroll and a prolonged couple of drinks. We returned about 10.00 pm in the dark and, crossing the second cattle-grid, the night-life scuttered away in the car lights. As we approached the house, the scene took on a foreboding look accompanied by the hoots of owls.

We got into bed and it sank in the middle like a hammock. The four posts swung inwards at the tops and outwards at the bottoms. How it supported us I don't know. The base of the bed was like an ancient wire mesh that could be tightened up with an adjusting key. Evidently, no further adjustment could be made, its lifespan had been reached. We slept very little with a tap, tap, tapping on the windows. It was only the tree branches. Or was it? They were indeed

an eerie and spooky two nights in a bed that offered no comfort or sleep in what we still to this day call 'Bella Lugosi's place.'

A fox jumped up one winter's night,
And begged the moon to give him light,
For he'd many miles to trot that night
Before he reached his den O!
Den O! Den O!
Before he reached his den O!

☐   The strangest bed I ever slept in was on a walking holiday in the Dales. On the road to Skipton, the railway runs alongside the road and small tunnels have been made under the railway banking for the farmers to get their machines through. As it got towards evening and we were looking for a place to sleep, I noticed a haycart under one of the tunnels. We made a little camp on the cart with the straw bales and laid out sleeping

Pontefract Museum

64

bags. We were quite cosy when we got used to the wind whistling through the tunnel.

☐ My dog, Rags, would never pass the graveyard without howling and tugging on his lead. He could sense something in there but I thought it was just because it was a churchyard. One day I took Rags into the graveyard to see if he could sniff out anything. Eventually, he started whining at one of these table graves which had a sunken side panel. As I peeped in, a horrible head slowly rose and turned to look at me. I was ready for running when the 'ghost' yelled, 'What time is it?' It turned out to be a woman tramp who had found a bed and had been sleeping there for a few weeks.

☐ My dad had a very tiring job and when he came home for his dinner at twelve o'clock, he would eat it quickly and go fast asleep in the chair beside the fire. One day I sat on his knee and with my new box of crayons, I coloured his face in different shades. He didn't feel a thing. At one o'clock my mother shouted, 'Come on Dad, have you seen the time?' He jumped up and ran out of the house to work.

When he came home that night, my mother said to him, 'What's happened to your face, Dad? Your forehead is blue and your chin is green.'

'Is it?' he said. 'No wonder everybody was staring at me on the tram.'

When he found out what I'd done, he didn't belt me. He was nice, my dad.

☐ In the 1920s I went on a walking holiday in Germany. There were eight of us and, when we came to our first night's lodging, we were split into twos. I was put with my sister as we were taken into a very old cottage and up a rickety staircase. Here were our bunk beds with very dirty straw filled mattresses in a tiny room.

'Will it have anything alive in it?' asked my sister.

'I don't care if it has,' I said, 'I'm too tired to bother.'

We climbed into bed with most of our clothes on and settled down to sleep. In the space below the room, we soon found out, were about ten cows with cowbells around their necks. Every time they moved, the bells rang. This went on until they settled down early in the morning. We were just dropping off when a cuckoo clock in the room started up. It cuckooed every fifteen minutes. What with the cowbells ringing and the cuckoo clock cucking, we didn't get a lot of sleep.

Pontefract and Castleford Express

— BUYING & ACQUIRING —

My father died a month ago
And left me all his riches;
A feather bed, and a wooden leg,
And a pair of leather breeches.

☐   My Auntie Alice has got the highest bed I've ever seen. It must be four foot off the bedroom floor. The reason is that she has three mattresses on the old sprung bedframe. Auntie Laura gave her them before she died and she can't bear to throw any of them out.

☐   We wanted to order a bed as a leaving present when Len left the Copperworks after thirty years service. We were told that a leaving present was usually something that never wore out; a clock, jewellery or glass. The man at the Co-op became rather indignant. 'I can assure you,' he maintained, 'that Co-op beds never wear out.'

☐   Beds became a subject of much embarrassment when I was about to get married. During the celebrations, people seem to become wicked and take a liking to sending wedding cards with condoms sellotaped to them. Some people came out with questions such as 'Are you a virgin?', 'Been on the nest lately?' 'Would you like to sit down? You'll be tired after all that sex.' Beds can bring the worst thoughts out in some people.

☐   A friend of mine had a spell of selling orthopaedic beds for a well known company. What he made in commission, he lost in expenses, often driving miles to find that a 'client' had sent in the enquiry form merely 'for a giggle.'

One evening he visited a middle-aged couple who seemed genuinely interested. She was a slight, wispy woman who complained of back trouble so he explained that the beds were all custom made. Perhaps one side could be sprung harder than the other to relieve her problem?

Eventually, the husband, a large, heavily built man, asked my friend if he would accompany him upstairs to take a look at their present bed, leaving the wife below to make tea. It was an oldfashioned model, sagging sadly in the centre and with brass rails at the head and foot.

'You definitely do need a new one,' said my friend with a grin, congratulating himself on almost certain commission.

'Aye, but can t'rails be still fixed to new 'un?'

'Well, I suppose so but most folks just buy a new headboard.'

'Nay, I must have a footrail. You see,' he lowered his voice, 'I'm used to them rails — need 'em for a bit of leverage when I'm on the job!' He tapped his nose and winked. 'Know what I mean?'

My friend now sells insurance.

☐   We once had a woman who turned up in fishnet stockings and a mini-skirt to demonstrate a water bed in the shop window. The bed started to leak, she got a soaking and by then a crowd had gathered outside the shop. They thought it was hilarious. The demonstrator drained the water from the bed, sealed the hole and continued with her display to loud cheers and applause from the, by then, big gathering. One young lad even came into the shop and asked if he might 'help' with the demonstration.

☐ You'd be surprised by what we get asked in a bed shop. I've been propositioned more than once. We regularly get people in complaining that their bed squeaks or requesting cushioning for the headboard because it bangs against the wall. One woman, who I know quite well, came in and complained that the castors on her bed broke after her husband took a flying leap from the top of the wardrobe!

☐ 'What was all that row about in your house last night?' Auntie asked. 'Why did you have the kids up until eleven o'clock?'

'It was our Willie causing a bloody stink up.' Willie was her seven year old son. 'He was shouting at his dad. You know Jack went for a pint last night and a game of dominoes?'

'Yes,' replied Auntie.

'Well, he came home and went to bed. He was feeling a bit frisky like. The bloody bed was rocking and rolling and squeaking like a nest of mice. Our Willie wakened up and came running into the bedroom shouting, 'What are you doing to our mam? What are you fighting for?'

'I got out of bed and bundled him back into his own but when I got back to our room, that big, slack pig had gone downstairs. He was fuming.

'I've a good mind to go upstairs and tan his arse for him.'

'You won't,' I said, the kid couldn't help it. Anyway keep off the bloody ale and help me to buy a new bed.'

'He did. It cost two shillings a week from the packy man.'

☐ We lived with Mother for a few months when we first got married. When we finally got a house and moved, we hoped that she would let us take the bed with us, the one we had been sleeping in. Mother said, 'You can only take the spring not the mattress.' We put old army coats and blankets and even a clipped rug on the spring to sleep on.

Not having a lot of money we went to an auction to buy our new bed. We ended up buying lot 29, an assortment of bed, chest of drawers, mop and bucket, all for £1.5s.0d.

☐ My daughter is very highly strung, so you can imagine what state her nerves were in when her very expensive bed got stuck in the middle of the stairs in her new home. My husband was at the top and coaxing it gently and Russ, my future son-in-law, was at the bottom, pushing and twisting the bed in different directions. All to no avail. It was just like a comedy sketch and tempers were flaring. My daughter screeched at them not to scratch the newly decorated staircase or spoil the bed. I just sat there open mouthed. This went on for over an hour. By this time, they had got it well and truly stuck. My husband was imprisoned in the middle of the stairs. There was no escape. There was nothing else to do but to get a saw and divide the bed into two portions. I only hope that it doesn't collapse when she is in it or else my husband, who is not in her good books, will really get the blunt end of her tongue.

☐ My mother always wanted a divan when they were in fashion but could never afford one so she decided to have a go at a bit of DIY. I came home from school to find that she had sawed off the foot of all the beds. Not with a saw but with a breadknife. It was the only thing that came to hand.

☐ When my husband's job forced us to move North, we bought the bed from the previous occupiers of the house we rented. We wondered at the time what they were going to sleep on. We found out to our cost when we moved South again two years later. The damn bed would not go through the window so we ended up bringing only the mattress South and leaving the base up North. Goodness knows what the next occupiers thought when they saw half a bed in their new bedroom.

☐ For months I kept telling my husband it's time we had a new bed. The one we slept on was 15 years old. There were creaks and groans from it and the sides were sagging but all my husband would say was, 'Oh! It's alright. It will last years yet.'

Passing by a bed shop I asked him to go in with me just to have a look round. It didn't need me to persuade my husband we needed a new bed. I just left it up to the salesman.

'Would you like to try this one, Sir?' he asked. Next thing my husband was lying on different beds. He finally decided on a lovely bed, with drawers and a really thick mattress. It was delivered a few days later.

I must say it took some getting used to this nice firm bed. We both ached all over for a few nights and I had to put up with my husband saying, 'I wish we had never got this new bed.' As time went on, we got used to it and it has all been worth while. We both think it was money well spent.

☐ Our old bed was well and truly worn out and the mattress was so soft that I needed a board under my side of the bed because I have a bad back. I bought a firm orthopaedic bed with a deep red dralon headboard and, when it arrived, my husband put it together and went out for a drink. I put on a nightie and threw myself headlong onto the bed and wham! I felt as if I was going to shatter into a thousand pieces. The mattress had no give in it at all. It was like diving onto a concrete slab. I heard my husband come in and, knowing what his reaction would be, I pretended to be asleep. He didn't disappoint me. His language was ripe and I got the distinct impression that this wasn't one of my better buys. Since I bought it he has slept on it no more than a dozen nights. The rest of the time he begs our nine year old daughter to swop places so that he can get a good night's sleep.

☐ The thing that appeals most of all to me about the bed trade is that it's a very clean trade, very few problems with it. Specially these days as people are getting more selective. More people are buying better beds; I think they're getting into the routine of wanting class. With instalment paying the difference between a bad bed and a good one is, only a few bob a week. People are realising at long last that they spend a third of their life in bed. Where else do you spend a third of your life?

A woman came in the shop one day and said, 'Can I have a look at your beds?' I showed her them and she turned up her nose and asked if I had anything more expensive. Normally you'd have to go to York or another large town to find a bed like the one she wanted but just to test her I said, 'I'll take you to the factory and you can lay on one.' To my surprise she agreed and bought one. It was a hand stitched, pocket sprung 'Imperial' — the Rolls Royce of beds. It cost her £850 and that's without a headboard. She paid cash. I wish I could sell one of them every week.

Val Green

—UPSTAIRS DOWNSTAIRS—

Tommy Trot, a man of law,
Sold his bed and lay upon straw;
Sold the straw and slept on grass,
To buy his wife a looking-glass.

☐ My grandad slept in a cupboard. When he lived with us his bed was in the living room behind two doors in the wall. The bed, which was inside, was pulled down at night and Grandad would settle into it. In the morning, he got up and pushed the bed back into the cupboard.

☐ Before we bought our Futon, we were discussing it in the office. Pam must have overheard part of the conversation and asked, 'Why don't you make your own?'

'I'm not very good at DIY,' I answered.

Well, it's only bits of fried bread, so what's your problem?'

☐ We stayed in Ardlui near Loch Lomond last year. It was an incredible place, full of suits of armour and stuffed animals. The bed was a magnificent four-poster with a mattress two foot thick. Beds are just beds now, but oh! how they used to be.

☐ This blow-up bed wasn't just a cheap lilo that you can blow up in a couple of minutes. It was a deluxe job, the same size as a proper double mattress, so it took a lot of air. The others had gone to bed. We went downstairs and tried to blow this thing up. We had a foot pump which didn't seem to make much impact on the mattress but certainly made lot of noise, a regular

thumping noise which went on for ages. They must have all heard it upstairs. When the thumping stopped, the giggling started. The combination must have finished them off. It took three quarters of an hour to pump it up and then it wasn't enough.

Lying on it was more difficult than blowing it up. It was alright if you stayed absolutely still but if you moved, the whole thing tilted and you started rolling off. It's difficult to combine laughing with sleeping.

☐ I used to love the oldfashioned beds; iron frames with big coil springs, covered by a mesh. About 40 years ago a friend of mine made a crystal and 'Cat's Whisker radio', which he used to listen to in bed. The aerial from the radio was fixed to the bed springs and he got very good reception from it.

☐ We got our first bed at a house sale in Ripon and it was beautiful; a rich mahogany with inlay, castors, metal legs and a chain-mail base. We couldn't afford it but in the end we decided to bid and the inevitable happened – it was ours.

To take it back to Barnsley we had to hire a van. I can remember what it said on the side to this day. 'Pennine Rent-A-Van.' Not a firm you often see in Ripon.

On the way back we were stopped at Ripley to have the tyres checked by a policeman who asked us rather pompously, 'Is this your van?' It wasn't but that didn't stop him declaring the tyres illegal.

It was the bed we started our family in. On the first night we warmed the room up but when Paul leapt onto the bed with great enthusiasm, the castors broke and it listed to one side. We spent the rest of the night on another secondhand bed in a cold, cold room.

Nine months later David was born.

☐ For years my 6ft 5 ins soldier husband had never slept in a bed long enough for his size. On his marriage to me in 1963, he applied on medical grounds and got a specially made, longer bed for our married quarters home. After years of sleeping with his knees up, he could now sleep contentedly at last.

The contentment didn't last long. For a start we had to put up with all sorts of innuendoes and jokes about our specially made bed. Then one night, with a loud creak, the metal soldering on our extension piece gave way and the bed collapsed. Of course, we had to put up with more teasing when the men arrived to repair it. And I was eight months pregnant at the time!

☐ I bought a king-sized bed and never gave a second thought as to how I was going to get it up the staircase of my two-up and two-down terrace house. It arrived two days later.

My husband had taken the afternoon off work so he could put the bed up. The delivery men jumped out of the van and proceeded to off-load the bed. Neither one of them was above 5ft 1ins.

I had this feeling things would not go as planned. It took ten minutes after opening the van doors to wrestle the mattress to a standstill as some idiot at the warehouse had tried to fold the mattress in half so it would fit easier into the van. Having taken the base into the bedroom, they then went to fetch the mattress. At that point, I knew things were definitely going wrong. The stairs, being all of 2½ feet wide and having a bend at the bottom of them, were in no way suitable for heaving a 5ft wide, 6ft long mattress up, not without breaking a few limbs in the process. To make matters worse, the walls were artexed, not the pretty patterned stuff either but the godawful spikey, arm lacerating type. The sort you learn not to fall onto no matter how drunk you are.

The delivery men were pushing and pulling for all they were worth but the bend at the bottom of the stairs wasn't going to let them through. After they had had a rest, they decided to give it one more go but it was no use. Meanwhile, I had made them a cup of coffee and was busy supplying painkillers and bandages to the slash marks on their arms. They then decided to fetch the boss and off they went. I'm still waiting for them coming back.

☐ We went on holiday in a caravan. Never having been in one before, it was all a bit strange. Me and my husband spent the week hanging on together in this 2' 6" bed. It wasn't until we were cleaning up to come home that we found it pulled out into a double bed.

☐ The bed would not go around the corner. It was a king-size Victorian bed, solid and heavy. We pushed, lifted, heaved, angled and shoved it and at last managed to get it to the second floor landing of the council flats. But we got stuck on a large wooden ball decorating a post. Whatever we did, we could not get past it.

After twenty minutes, we did the only thing we could. We sawed off the ball.

☐ People are going back to iron or brass bedsteads now but it's just a passing phase. Then there's pocket sprung, poster sprung, open coil, the ultimate sleep system and the continuous springs – that's the hippopotamus and duck bed.

☐ We'd just moved in to a farmhouse with a beamed bedroom, 26 feet by 22 feet, when we met a guy who made waterbeds. There's a shop in the Bond Street Centre in Leeds, The Dream Merchants I think it's called, and we copied one in there. It cost £11,000 there, mind you, while we did it for £420. It's seven foot square and we had to have a quilt made specially. It cost 60p a week to run and the only problem we had was when the heater conked. We had to evacuate then and go and sleep somewhere else. It takes a week to warm the bloody thing up.

I had a labrador and a Springer spaniel and my wife had two Persian cats. They were learning to live with each other at the same time as we were. When the bedroom door opened in the morning it was a race to see who could get on the bed first.

At Christmas we gave a housewarming party and the whole amateur operatic society my wife's in — that's 15 people — were bouncing on the bed together.

☐ My sister and I had a rather eccentric aunt and uncle. Sometimes, usually before Christmas, we would go to stay there for a week or so. We looked forward to it as we enjoyed some things we didn't get at home. There were lots of different children to play with, warm macaroons just out of the oven,

mushy peas with vinegar, a battered old ginger cat always asleep on the sofa and an old clock with a wonderful slow tick-tock in our bedroom.

After *The Archers* on the wireless and a quick wipe with a damp cloth, another thing we liked because we were never expected to have a proper wash, it was upstairs to bed. We said prayers, then climbed into bed whilst Aunty wound the clock up. Then with a 'Goodnight, God Bless,' it was off to sleep.

I always had difficulty getting to sleep. The bed was an old flock mattress covered by a well-patched sheet. On top of another well-patched sheet was a motley collection of old coats, crochet shawls, travelling rugs and anything else that would keep us warm. The pillows felt as if they were stuffed with cut up materials, flocks and feathers. The bed itself turned out to be two singles pushed together, thus having a hard wooden centre.

Usually we slept well once we got to sleep, helped by the tick-tock of the old clock. One

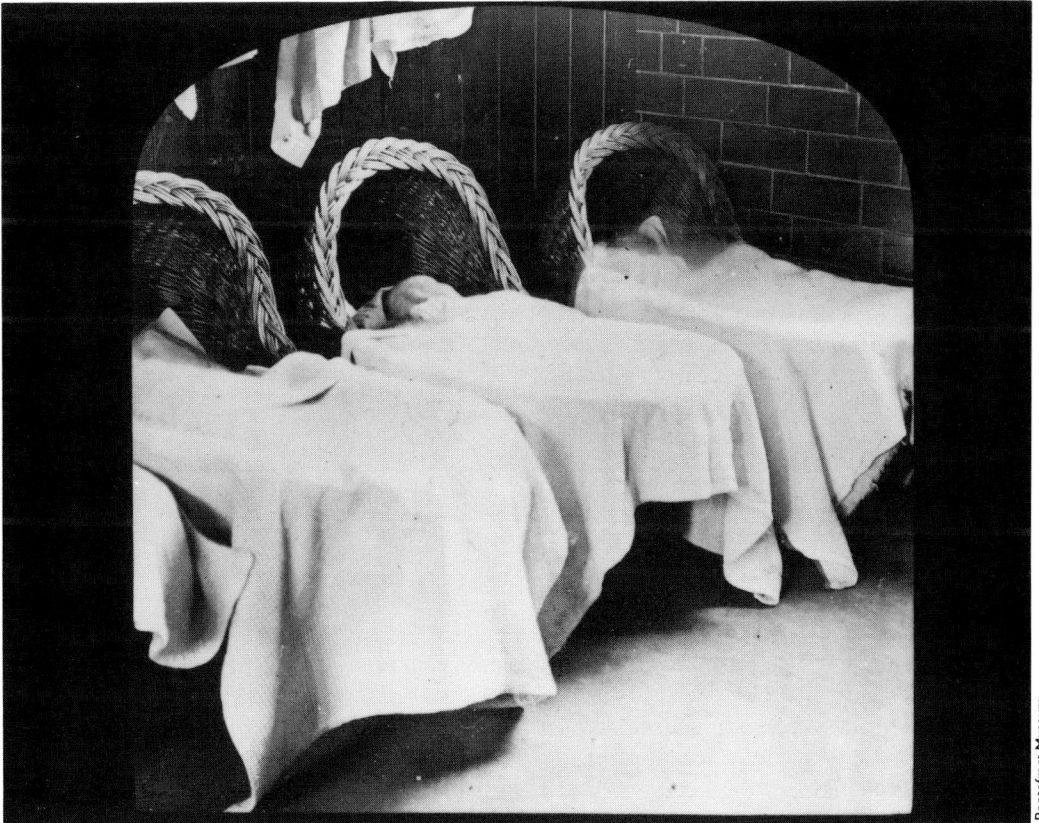

Pontefract Museum

night my bed seemed unusually lumpy and hard and I found it impossible to get to sleep. By the light of the small night candle, which was always left in the bedroom overnight, I decided to find out what the lumps were. Feeling inside the mattress cover, which was merely folded over at the end and not even sewn, I pulled out a number of cut up coats, some still with buttons attached, and then I got to the real lumps. Bars of soap, lots of them, all new and still in their packets. Some were packs of two, three or four. As a five year old I thought my aunt had probably lost them and would be pleased with me for finding them. I collected all the soap from the mattress and more from under the pillow and piled it all up at the side of the bed until morning.

In the morning I proudly showed my aunt what I had found. She just giggled and giggled. Some time later, after she'd recovered from her fit of the giggles, she explained that it made the beds smell nice and all the beds in the house had soap in them. She also told me that the soap dried out the longer it was kept. The more it dried out the longer it lasted.

Thirty years later, when it fell to my sister and me to clear the house out, we collected a large box of soap from all over the house as well as from the beds.

☐ When I was pregnant, you wore the clothes you had. If it was a skirt, you had a piece of elastic pulling from the button across to the button hole to make it fit at the waist. As time went on the bed was brought downstairs into the living room. Aunty could hardly manage going up and down the stairs because of her arthritis and she was a big woman, so having the bed downstairs was helpful for her to look after me. You didn't go into hospital like they do now if they thought you were alright because what was wrong with you was that you were pregnant. They used to blame being pregnant if they

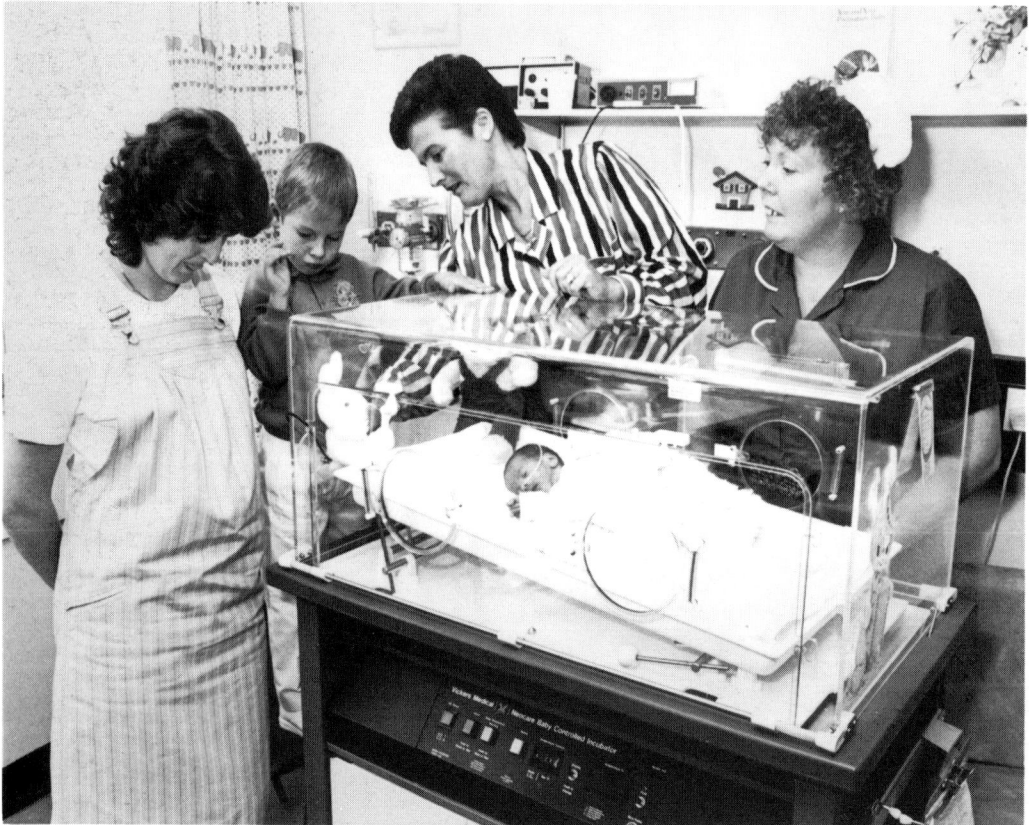

Pontefract and Castleford Express

couldn't pay the soddin rent some of them.

The bed was a big oldfashioned four-poster, a spring mattress and a flock bed, which had to be tossed up and down to work the flock free from big lumps. If you didn't do this properly and went to sleep it used to get very hard so God help you if you didn't get it right. Uncle used to say it was like sleeping on Hill 60 in the First War.

☐   My first baby's cot was a washing basket. We were living at my mother's house and didn't have much room. The basket was ideal; he looked so cosy in it and it was easy to move around the house with it.

☐   I have always had great control when breaking wind. A few years ago, I went to see the Rugby League Cup Final at Wembley with two mates. We decided to stay for the weekend and found a reasonable hotel in Sussex Gardens. Apparently, on Saturday night when we returned from a good night out and we had settled down for the night, according to old Bob, I was soon at it.

Seemingly fast asleep I was performing loud and long at regular intervals. Bob was fascinated. He stayed awake for two nights laughing at my performance, not daring to sleep lest he missed something. It was, he says, one of his most enjoyable weekends out with the lads.

His favourite story lasted him many more years in the snap cabin. He always grabbed the attention with his opening words, 'I know a bloke who can fart in his sleep.'

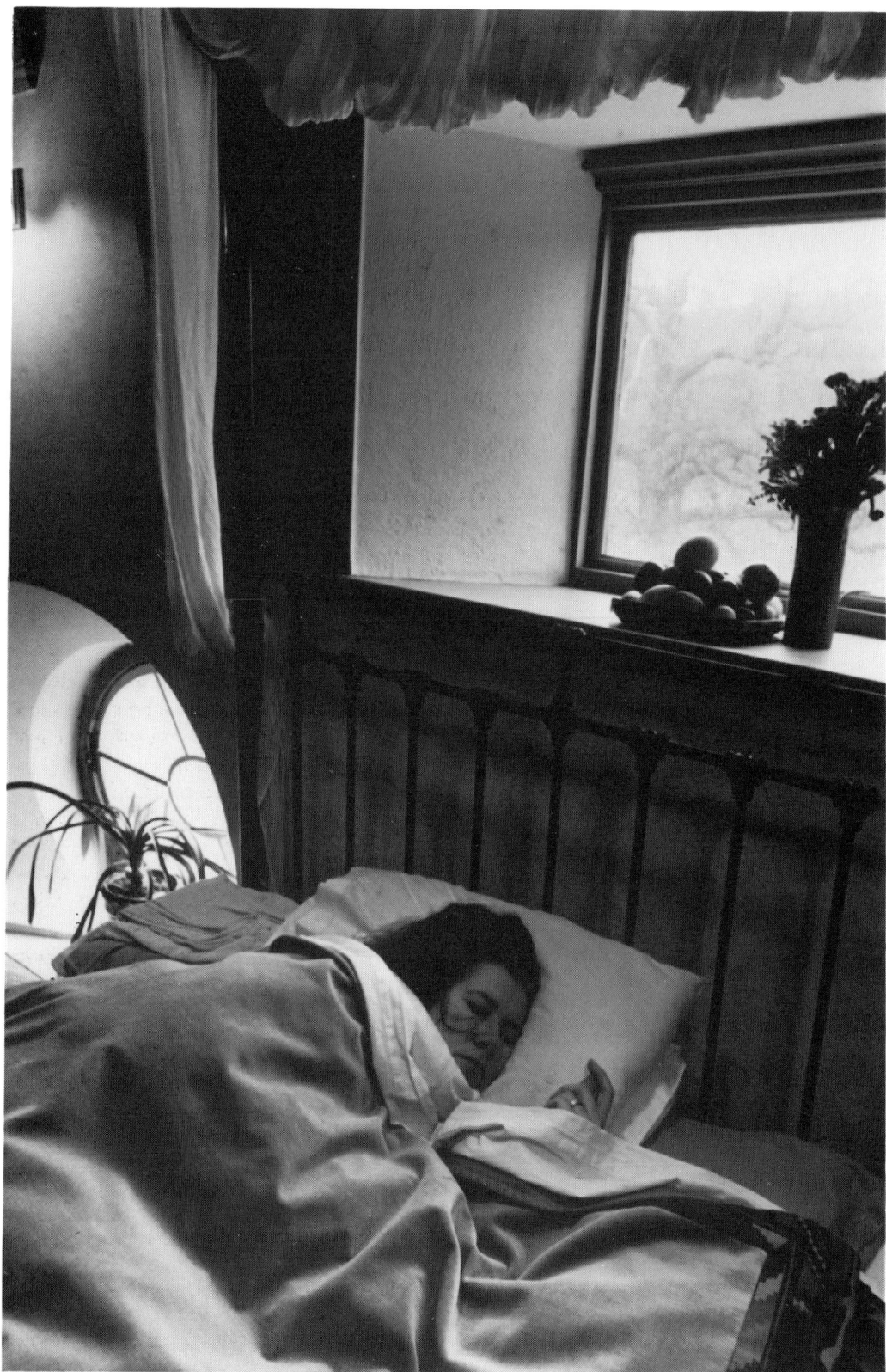

BEDTIME

There were three in a bed and the little one
said,

'Roll over, roll over.'

So they all rolled over and one fell out.

There were two in a bed and the little one said,

'Roll over, roll over.'

So they all rolled over and one fell out.

And the little one said, 'Good night, good night.'

☐ I slept in bed with my sister until I was 21. We were only apart twice. Her first holiday from me happened because I was given a halfpenny to spend. My brother tried to steal it so I put it in my mouth and swallowed it. I ended up in hospital until it passed through my system. My sister's second respite from me was when I got St Vitus Dance and I couldn't stop jerking so I had to sleep in a bed downstairs. I enjoyed sleeping with my sister, playing I spy and dancing to songs and records. Radio Luxembourg was a big part of our lives as we became teenagers.

☐ I suppose a lot of men fantasise about going to bed with two women. I once had the experience and I didn't enjoy it much at all. I was full of cold at the time and laid on the sofa as miserable as sin. Julie's mate, Stephanie, was round at our house and they were poking fun at me. Then straight out of the blue, Stephanie says, 'I know how we can cheer him up,' and she whispered something to Julie.

They both giggled and started to undress. Then they told me to follow them to the bedroom. I was like a dog with two dicks but at the same time I didn't know where to put myself. I'm embarrassed to say it now but I got that excited I came straight away and I just couldn't get another erection, even when they started to play about with one another. In the end, I went back to the sofa sniffling and left them to it. It didn't cheer me up at all.

☐ There is a tendency with Indians to sleep together. We go to bed to sleep when we are tired. None of this English idea about being 'sent to bed' or 'bedtime.'

☐ A good friend of mine always maintained that she never dreamed. 'It's not that you don't dream,' I argued, 'you just don't remember them.'

'No,' she insisted, 'I never dream.'

A couple of years ago we decided to visit the Edinburgh Festival together. We stayed for five nights in the halls of residence at one of the Edinburgh colleges which takes paying guests during the summer.

I always have difficulty getting to sleep in strange beds and so I was usually still lying awake after my friend had dropped off to sleep. The first night, I heard her moving around and when I looked over she was kneeling on the floor looking under her bed.

'What are you doing?' I asked her.

'I'm looking for the jewels,' she answered.

She seemed so positive that it didn't immediately occur to me that she was still asleep. As I continued to talk to her she rambled on about the hidden treasure and got back into bed where she remained for the rest of the night.

The next morning I took great pleasure in recounting to her the night's activities and was met by complete disbelief. Nothing I said could persuade her I was telling the truth.

What I took to be an isolated incident prompted by the subconscious trauma of being in a strange bed in a strange room turned out to be a nightly series. After the second night when she sat bolt upright in bed and banged her head on the wallmounted bookshelf above, and the third night's sitting up in bed peering out of the window to see what the weather was like and to chat with the owls, I began to suspect that this was the rule rather than the exception. Half remembered stories of horrific crimes committed by sleepwalkers flitted through my mind and I had visions of awaking to find my friend standing over me armed with an axe.

The interruptions continued, however, in a much more sedate and edifying form. I will never forget the extremely lengthy and articulate criticism she delivered of an exhibition of Scottish pipes. Whether plumbing or musical was never clear, for we had not visited any such event.

She continued to deny indignantly that she even dreamed, let alone talked and walked in her sleep, and my claims went unsupported until she fell in love. Early on in their new relationship her partner asked her if he could attend a music workshop she was running, so he could see her at work. She refused saying he'd make her nervous and distract her. A few days later, however, he told her, 'I don't have to come to the workshops now, you did the whole thing for me in your sleep last night.'

☐ Before we came to England we lived in Mabala, Uganda. A rich old lady lived near us in a big house and when her sons went away, my sister, brother and me went to stay with her because she was frightened to be on her own. Everybody knew she had lots of money and a lot of people said she had jewels and gold. When we were in bed one night, some robbers came to get the old lady's gold. We hid under the bed but we could see them with their big swords out. It was really scary,

especially when we realised that our father could not help us because the thieves had put a big stopper across the door to our house and locked him in.

☐ During the war, when I was a young girl, my family kept the local pub. On one occasion a Canadian RAF man was there celebrating his 21st birthday. He was staying the night in the best bedroom, where two of my sisters had made up an apple-pie bed and filled it with brooms and all sorts of rubbish. I was asleep in the room next door but not for long. As soon as the man got into his bed and found out what had been done to it, he leapt out again and into bed with me. So I slept with a Canadian at the tender age of five!

☐ Quickly, we dived on to the bed. Its springs creaked and groaned to protest as we snuggled under the eiderdown, cold toes searching for equally cold toes, their touch bringing warmth and reassurance as we gazed at the ceiling, silent and afraid, the urgent whine of the sirens replaced by the menacing drone of the planes flying overhead.

'Cocoa's ready,' Mum declared and four eager pairs of hands reached upwards for the comforting mugs of warmth and nourishment.

'Tell us about Uncle Raymond, when he put the chickens on the duck pond to swim, Mum,' said our Frank, the cheekiest and most daring of all of us. We gazed in rapture as Mum, gently rocking by the fireside, the glow making a halo of her auburn hair, began the story we loved to hear. Words were already spilling over in our minds, pictures setting the scene before Mum could utter a word. Like children from time immemorial we thirsted for the old familiar words to be repeated over and over again. Mum smiled at us from her rocking chair, the warmth and cosiness had almost sent us back to sleep.

We all said a special prayer for our Dad who was at work making 'chucks' for aeroplanes. I never did find out what 'chucks' were but they must have been important because he didn't have to be a soldier.

Outside nation was fighting against nation but for me this time of strife will always be remembered with joy. Was that cold, dark cellar such a magical place? I think not. The magic was surely in the love of our mother, who, alone and afraid, transformed a time of fear and anxiety into a warm oasis which will be forever in my mind.

I lost my virginity at 13 in a derelict air-raid shelter in Hull. We did it on a badly vandalised bus seat and it lasted about two minutes. In fact, in about the space of ten minutes, Dave, Peter and Christopher lost their virginity as well. We all queued up. I think I came first.

Suzanne was a short, dumpy girl with bright red hair and freckles. She said that we hadn't to tell anybody in case her mother found out. Of course, we couldn't wait to brag to our mates.

I saw Suzanne about ten years later. She was absolutely beautiful, like a Pre-Raphaelite woman. She didn't recognise me.

☐ My father was a strict man, a Sergeant Major. One Saturday night he said to me, 'When I call you in the morning you must come down straightaway or I will be up with my jug of water.'

When I got upstairs I asked my sister if I could sleep in her bed. I told her I wanted a change.

Next morning I heard his loud voice at the stairs' door. 'May! May! May!' he shouted. I turned over and went back to sleep. He came running upstairs with his jug and half-drowned my sister before he realised that I'd tricked him.

When I came home from church I was told to get undressed and go to bed for the rest of the day, and I got the same treatment when I came home from school the next day as well.

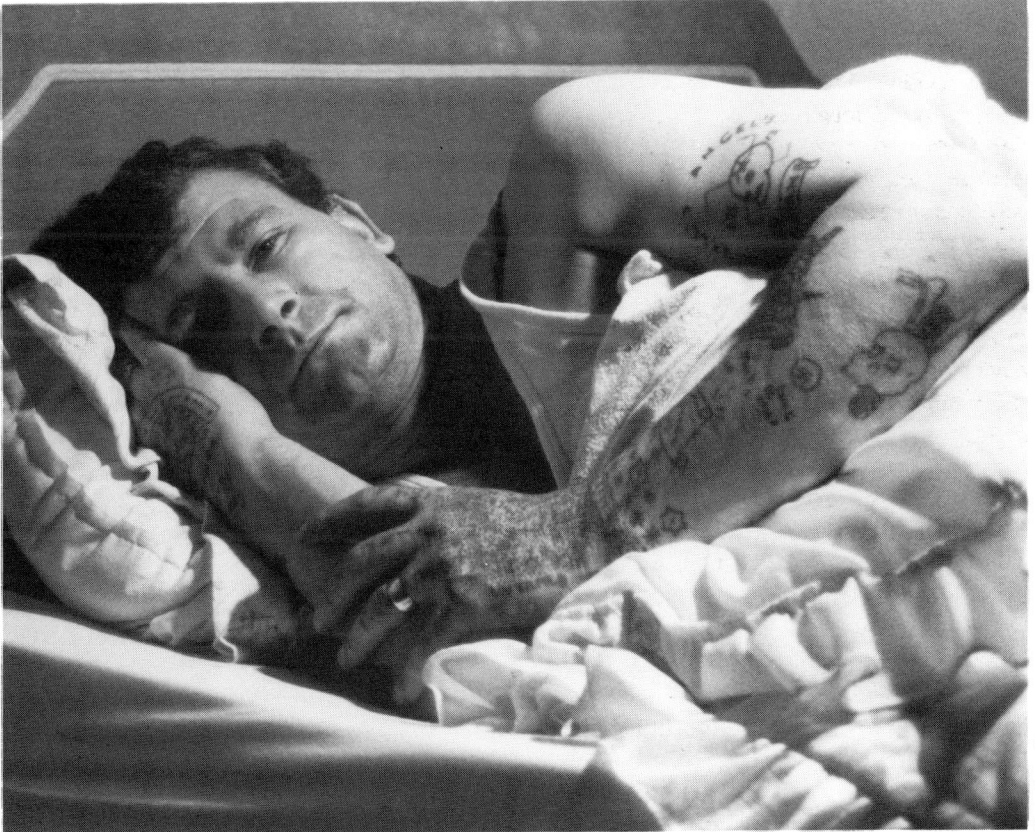

Kevin Reynolds

□ I was the middle one of five girls and a bit of a rebel. I often drove my sweet-natured mother mad with my bad behaviour.

'Get up those stairs and stay there, until you can behave yourself,' she said one day.

I went up to the room I shared with my sister and sat on the bed. Within minutes I was bored and looking for something to do. I wound up the gramophone my grandmother had given us and put on a record of a woman singing *Ramona*.

My imagination took flight and in the available space in the room I danced Isadora Duncan fashion until the record ended. I enjoyed doing that. Apparently, my parents could hear what I was up to and had a good laugh. They secretly admired my spirit but knew very well it had to be curbed at times.

□ I was causing trouble again. My sisters and I had been in bed for some time and I could not sleep so I kept my sisters awake. After a while, Dad called from the stairs bottom that he would come up and 'crack my arse' if I didn't behave.

Five minutes later, when the noise was even greater, he came upstairs, carrying the flickering candle which was housed in a Wee Willie Winkie type candle holder. He threw back the covers and smacked my backside.

When he'd gone back downstairs, I felt something on my face and hair. I was terrified. I'd heard stories of bedbugs and was sure they were attacking me. It turned out to be candle grease.

□ Sex was never mentioned in my presence and I naively thought that as my mother was a widow she led a celibate life. I suppose, in hindsight, my ignorance was really bliss.

I'd be about ten years old when I started to be inquisitive about the mysterious rubber and glass object that for years had lain alongside our best fruit spoons in Mother's sideboard drawer. This 'thing' had a bright orange rubber bulb attached to a glass end piece which flared out widely at the end.

As my mother was very strict, I knew better than to ask what it was for, so one day

I asked my sister. She replied, 'I think it's for when you get constipated. They stick it up your bum and then it sucks the awkward bits out.'

I was horrified at the mere thought of it and always made sure I never had to suffer such torture, for that was what it sounded like to me.

It has always seemed odd that this contraption had lain alongside my mother's best fluted fruit spoons and yet I never remember anyone knowing what it was for. Years later I found out from a nurse that it was a contraceptive device called a 'douche.'

□ The Higginson's syringe was a strange piece of equipment. I discovered this weird and wonderful thing wrapped in a towel on the bedside table in my parents' bedroom. The syringe was made of black rubber, about eighteen inches long and sported an ivory nozzle at one end. In the middle of the rubber tubing was a balloon shaped area. The balloon was the pump and when the end of the syringe was inserted in water, the pump was squeezed and released, thus filling the syringe with water in readiness for use.

The Higgingson's syringe was a rudimentary form of contraception. Its efficiency can be judged by the fact that I am one of six children.

Off to bed, sleepy head

Tarry a while, says slow.

Put on the pot, says greedy gut,

We'll sup before we go.

□ Auntie Beryl was our very special auntie. She didn't have a husband and she used to come on Friday nights. We couldn't wait for her to undo the bag of sweets she always brought. When we'd had our faces washed and were made ready for bed, we'd fetch the Janet and John books down. We used to sit in front of the fire and she'd put her arms round us and squeeze us up. She couldn't turn the pages over. Two sisters vying for attention, it was a real bun fight.

☐ I was married recently to a man who has a sixteen year old daughter. We realised that it might be hard for her to have a stepmother, but, touch wood, things are going well.

When we go to bed, she trots off to her room but feels confident enough to come to our bedroom without warning. It makes me feel good that she does that. If she'd been different, I would have found it hard.

☐ Going out was a treat when we had three children and we had a good babysitter who would look after the children when we could manage to go. We would put the kids to bed before we went out and they would promise to be good.

'Oh, they've been no trouble,' she would say when we got back.

It was years later she told us that they had pillow fights and great lannekins before they went to sleep.

☐ I used to do anything to stay up at night. After being bathed and got ready for bed, I would start to darn my stockings and, even though I didn't like doing it, I would offer to darn anybody else's that needed doing as well.

I would brush my hair, over and over, learn to knit and sew, sitting quietly on the sofa hoping Dad wouldn't notice me. But sure enough, he would, and off to bed I would have to go.

When I got married and had my own children, I realised that the only peace parents have is when the kids are safely tucked up in bed.

☐ I was never told bedtime stories because my mother said, 'By the time bedtime comes along, I've seen enough of you.'

☐ All the other kids made fun of us because we had to suffer the shame and indignity of always being the first children in our street to have to go to bed. Of course, early to bed meant we were always the first up as well so we were tired out by half past

seven anyway. We would sit on the settee and pretend to be as awake as possible. Our dad judged our readiness for bed by how often we rubbed our eyes or yawned. Every time I felt the urge to yawn or rub my eyes, I would lean over the edge of the sofa in the hope he wouldn't notice.

☐ I don't care about bedtime as a concept. Last night I watched the telly until 3 am then did some washing and ironed while I was listening to some records. My clocks are all at the wrong time so I don't have alarm clocks. I open the curtains slightly, that's my alarm clock. I don't care about going to bed sometimes either. If I'm that way out, I just curl up on my sofa or on the rug in front of the gas fire.

☐ I hardly ever bother with sleeping since Sky television came in. I stop up till three and four watching. I know most of it is a load of shit but I'm addicted.

☐ Going to bed the French way was a favourite. We'd throw ourselves backwards with our legs in the air. Then there was the Japanese and the Greek way. We'd spend hours playing that game, making up ways of going to bed like different nationalities.

There was an old woman who lived in a shoe,
She had so many children she didn't know what to do;
She gave them some broth without any bread;
She whipped them all soundly and put them to bed.

☐ When we first got BBC2, Dad was very proud. The aerial looked different from the others and was something of a status symbol. It meant we could watch *Call My Bluff* and posh documentaries and Dad could watch sophisticated French films with sub-titles. I always wondered at the time why Dad watched the French films. For one thing he didn't speak French and for another he couldn't read.

Best of all, though, *The High Chapparal*, a popular western at the time, was on BBC2. I had to go to bed before it started but I always made sure I caused enough trouble so that they'd ask me to come downstairs. Punishment was to stand in the corner of the front room until presumably I became tired. I had worked it out, though, that I could watch the TV through the reflection in our china cabinet and of course I could hear the soundtrack. I am still an expert on characters and storyline in *High Chapparal*.

☐ We often used to have pillow-fights. These would always start off as great fun but, after a while, we would begin to get a bit rougher and hit just a little bit harder until we ended up having a full scale fight. Then we would be sent to our own separate bedrooms to think about saying sorry to each other.

☐ Me and my sister shared a big double bed. I liked having my feet tickled and I used to lay at one end of the bed and my sister at the other and I used to offer her some of my pocket-money if she would tickle my feet. We would often fall out.

'You're going to sleep,' I would say as she stopped tickling my feet.

'You've stopped as well,' she'd say because I would have to tickle my sister's foot in exchange.

☐ We fought a nightly battle because I loved to read at least for as long as I was allowed to and usually a good bit longer, whereas my sister insisted that she could not sleep if the light was on. Of course, she would tell on me if I switched the light back on after official bedtime. Once I took revenge by convincing her, on the eve of her first communion, that she had red spots on the soles of her feet which were a symptom of black typhoid and that her life was in grave danger. Throughout the build-up towards her big day, my sister was quite susceptible and I could be very plausible so

late on the eve of her communion, my mother had to reassure a distraught and sobbing ten year old that her twelve year old sister had made it all up.

☐ The kids never go to bed on time. They mess around and make excuses. They're always up and down, up and down, especially Jennifer. When she was young she never used to go to sleep. She was hyperactive. She'd be put to bed but she'd start taking all the clothes off her teddies and pull all the stuff out of the wardrobe and empty drawers. She'd wreck the bedroom. Eventually, she'd wear herself out and fall asleep for about an hour and then it was time to get up.

☐ They call it 'hyperactive' these days. When I was a kid they called it 'being a bloody nuisance.' My parents screwed my cot to the bedroom floor and put iron bars at the window because they once found me outside on the windowsill. They tied the doorknob to the bannister rail after I once escaped and climbed up the chimney.

☐ I never throw away bed sheets that have worn in the middle. Out of the good pieces, I make pillowcases, dusters, cot sheets and lots of other things.

☐ What a terrible chore I used to find changing a duvet cover. It really used to tow me to death until one day I realised if I turn the cover inside out with hands at each corner, grab hold of the duvet and shake it down, the job I used to hate turns out to be very simple.

☐ Our little bedroom, as we first called it, was gradually being converted into a bathroom. First a sink, then a bath and finally a toilet. My bed was in this room so I eventually slept in the bathroom.

☐ There is a ghost at the hotel who used to be a cleaner called Tom. There's a picture of him in one of the corridors. He used to carry a coin between his nose and his chin. A lass who worked here before saw him on a bed in room seventeen. He goes in wardrobes an' all. Sometimes they just won't open. You writhe at it and we'd say, 'Come on Tom, let go' or owt like that, just as a joke like, and it would open. I have never seen him but you know when he's around. It goes right cold.

☐ Me and my friend Barbara were working in London in a hotel in Bayswater and we were given accommodation in this big old house with rooms for staff. We were given a big room to share which contained an old, faded, fitted carpet, an old fireplace, a couple of chairs, a table and two beds. The beds were pushed into opposite corners of the room and one was definitely on its last legs. They were small single beds and we decided to toss a coin to see who would get the better bed. Well, I lost the toss and that night I got into the bed and it sank in the middle. It was like sleeping in a hammock. The next day I was bent double with a bad

back. Barbara couldn't stop laughing until I said we would have to take turns and share the good bed. Anyway, I ended up making the hammock into a bed on the floor and it was a damn sight more comfortable.

Ladybird, ladybird, fly away home,

Your house is on fire, your children at home;

One is upstairs making the beds,

The others downstairs are crying for bread.

☐ During the war I was an air-raid warden and had to get out of bed at night when the siren went, looking for fires. One night I scrambled into my clothes as the wail of the siren sounded and set off out into the dark night. I wandered round the town until the all clear went and started for home. As I reached our street, I saw a reddish glow coming from one of the windows. I hadn't heard any bombs dropping but this looked

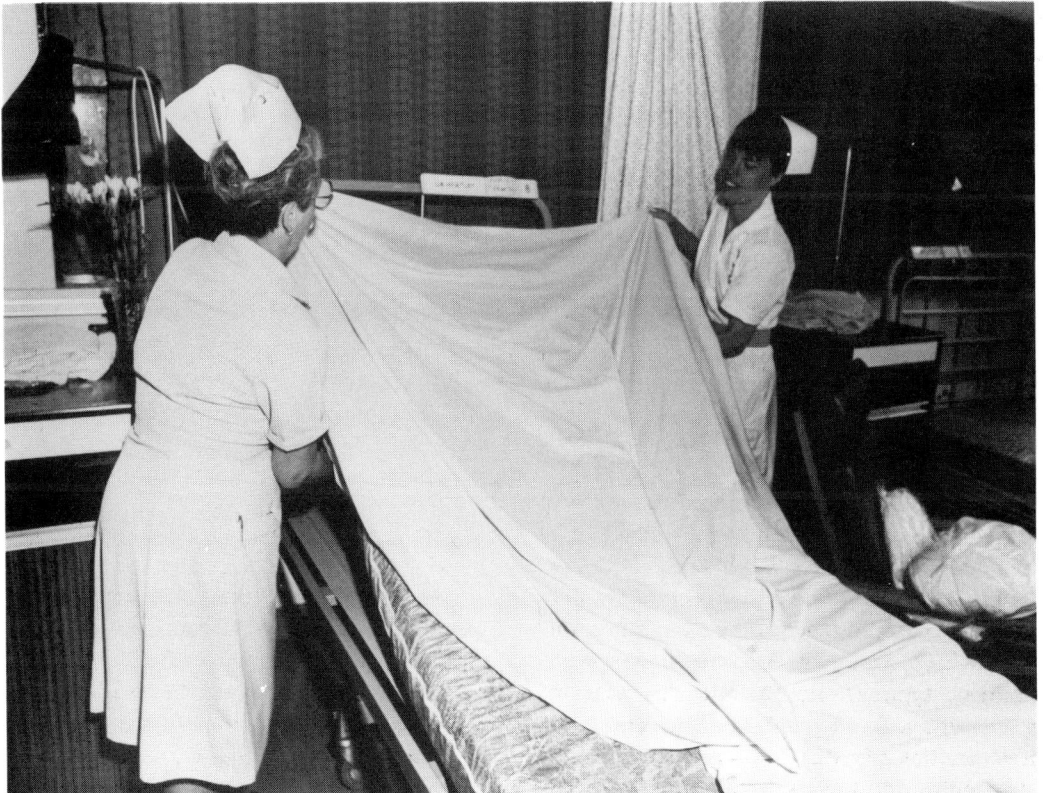

Val Green

like a fire. I decided to investigate. There looked to be a real blaze inside as I approached the window and I was just about to blow my whistle, when I thought I would peep through a crack in the curtains. There was a roaring fire alright and in the rosy glow of the firelight were my neighbours, vigorously making love on the floor, totally unaware that there had been an air-raid. It's a good job I didn't blow my whistle.

☐ My two brothers and me hated bonfire nights because we had to watch the fire and fireworks from the bedroom window. All the other children in the area used to poke fun at us because we weren't allowed out. We used to plead to be allowed out to join in but to no avail. My two brothers had been quite badly burned in separate incidents so our parents would not give in. Tony had his scalp burned when a catherine wheel flew off its nail and spun round on his head and Andrew's arm was badly injured when an aeroplane struck him.

☐ My boyfriend was in the army and a soldier in the same sleeping quarters as him always kept everyone else awake at night with his snoring. They suffered for months trying everything they could think of to stop it so they could get a decent night's sleep but no luck. Then they decided to take the snoring soldier, complete with bed, out of the hut in an attempt to get some sleep. When the really loud snores started they all got up. The soldier slept so soundly he didn't even wake up when they dropped the bed as they took it down two steps out of the hut.

☐ When I was an air-raid warden, I always told the Chief that I couldn't sleep when I was on call. Waiting for the sirens and the slightest noise kept me awake. One night the siren went off and I went to the headquarters which was a small hut with a table, telephone and two bunks. When I arrived, I was the first in so I climbed onto the top bunk and fell asleep. When I woke up the all clear was just sounding.

'Thy hasn't done bad to say tha can't sleep,' said the Chief. 'Tha's slept through two hours of bombing.'

☐ The noise of the clock startled me. I was just falling off to sleep when it struck two in the morning. I was staying at a friend's house. We were going on the club trip by ourselves the next morning. We were both sixteen and very excited. Veronica's mother and father were snoring their heads off in the next room.

It was the first time our parents had trusted us to go on our own without their supervision. I laid quite still for a while then I felt someone shaking me.

'June, June are you asleep?'

'No,' I whispered. 'I'm too excited about Blackpool to be able to sleep.'

'Shall we have a fag?' asked Veronica.

'Your mam will smell it, won't she?'

'No, I'll open the window. And I've got a jewellery box here for the tab ends.'

By the time we'd wafted clouds of smoke and smoked three cigs a piece, the bedroom smelt of stale tobacco. Veronica had to put the tab ends in the old tin jewellery box and shoved it as far under the bed as she could get it, saying, 'Me mam doesn't go under beds that often, I'll shift it before she finds it.'

We had a great time at Blackpool the next day but it wasn't so good when we had to face the music on the night when we got back to Veronica's. Olive, Veronica's mum, was waiting for us at the top of the entry where they lived.

'Have you enjoyed yourselves then you two buggers?' She gave us a clip on the head as we tried to dodge past her. We knew what had happened. Veronica's mum had found the tab ends tucked safely under the bed.

☐ He was a very quiet man, my dad's brother, not much good at conversation. The only time he did have anything to say was the day he came back from his holidays. He would tell us every detail and then that was it for another year.

As usual, he bid us all goodnight and off he

went to bed. About an hour later he came downstairs, filled a pot of water and went back up to bed. A couple of minutes later he got another pot full. He did this about four times. We sat there wondering what the hell he was up to.

In the end my mother couldn't stand the suspense. She said, 'What's all the water for, Harry?' as he went through the hall door.

'Don't worry, it's only the bed. It's on fire.'

☐ We like to burn jos sticks to make our bedroom smell nice. We once set fire to the mattress by lighting them. We threw the mattress out of the window and the fire brigade came. That was at a lady's house in Nairobi.

☐ In Nigeria you can get a bit frightened to go to sleep because of the lizards and snakes. When you get up in the morning you can see them sunbathing on the garden wall. The best thing to do with a snake or a lizard is to pick it up by its tail and bang it on a stone.

☐ You can usually lie down and see little lizards on the ceiling in Pakistan. If they come near my bed, I shoo them away. Mostly, though, we sleep outside in the summer at home, under the sky.

☐ My Grandma and Auntie used to tell me a lot of bedtime stories and I try to tell them to my children. One was about a little bird who fetched some rice and dahl to make a kedgeree and then put it in a chika so no cats or animals could get to it. My children always laugh when I say 'chika' because it seems such an oldfashioned word to them. Chika was what we used back home in Pakistan to keep things cool before fridges.

☐ My grandma used to give me cocoa. She liked me better than the others and so she spoiled me. Her bed smelt musty because it wasn't slept in very often but I liked that smell. My grandad told stories that he made up about me. It made me feel important.

☐ Mum left me asleep in bed when she went to the shops on Saturday morning. Invariably, I would wake up because by instinct I knew she wasn't there. I would be heartbroken and would stand at the kitchen window, crying and thinking she wouldn't come back. I did that every Saturday until I saw her coming round the corner of the street.

☐ I would never 'send' my children to bed. I think it's very cruel.

☐ Kids go to their rooms voluntarily now. Since home computers and central heating became popular you can't keep them out. Dad wouldn't have let us put posters up. Pictures had to be put up properly in our house. I like my kids to decorate their rooms with things. They're into wildlife posters at the moment.

☐ Lorry drivers have a code of honour. They offer each other a bed when they go to their friend's house. My dad's mate ended up in Bradford one night and my sister gave up her bedroom for him. She had a Cliff Richard poster on the wall from *Summer Holiday*. Cliff was leaping in the air. The lorry driver woke up in the middle of the night and couldn't picture where he was and saw Cliff. He thought someone was flying at him and screamed.

I suppose it would have tickled Cliff if he knew he'd scared a big brawny lorry driver.

BEDROOMS

☐ Garfield is a popular bedroom paper but then it is also a good paper to put in the lavatory; any place where people have time to read. Children like it and so do adults but that's probably because lines like 'Nothink as loving as somethink taken from the oven' have a universal appeal.

☐ When I was young, about three years old, my friend was staying. We were in bunk beds. I remember daring her to put her head through the bars at the end of the bed. She took me up on it but she got her head stuck. She lay there for about half an hour. I didn't believe her until she started screaming and then Mum and Dad came up and spent the rest of the evening with soap and water trying to get her head out.

☐ My daughter was playing upstairs with a friend. I thought they were very quiet so I went up to investigate and found my daugher fastened to the bed knob by her wrists. I had to cut her free with a knife because her wrists were beginning to swell.

☐ To me no bed is as comfortable as a feather bed. I don't think they are made now but my boyfriend's mother had them. I loved to sleep in one. The bedrooms were very big and sometimes very cold but a coal fire could be made in the small fireplace in the bedroom, lovely and warm and cosy.

☐ My ideal bedroom for a start would be as far from my sister's as possible. It would have a sink so I could have a drink. The bedroom would be quite big and would have lots of hiding places. I'd have a cabin bed. I would also like to have a lego table big enough to build a whole town on. It would have a secret staircase to a science lab. The lab would have lots of strange things in it, things like potions that made lego men become real. I'd have a robot that went around picking things up and putting them in their place. The carpet would be green. The wallpaper would have blue, red and yellow all over. I'd have one big chest of drawers to put all my toys in. Next to the cabin bed there would be a computer that you typed in the book you wanted to read and the book would come out of a slit in the wall.

☐ My bedroom is bigger than my brother's. I share it with my sister but I have a wardrobe and a cabin bed. When we first got it I thought that the wood had eyes which looked at me and I was frightened. My dad said they were only knots in the wood but I wanted him to hang something over them so he put up a wallhanging with rabbits on it.

There are lots of nice things and you can play hide and seek in it. The best place to hide is behind the desk under the cabin bed. Sometimes my best friend, Fiona, and me go into this hiding place, we switch a torch on and stay there for hours. I have little curtains and a separate area where my fast food kitchen is.

☐ My bedroom is all my own. It is just great for what I need. It is neatly decorated, like an office, with shelves to accommodate my many books and files. It is my private thinking place. It is painted green with a sage green carpet and black ash furniture. There I sleep and do lots of school homework. I have a midi hi-fi which I love and listen to all the time. My Mum is always complaining because I never turn it off. I draw a lot on my drawing board, which is fixed in my room. I think of my bedroom as my private workplace in which I compute, write stories and assignments for school. I also write my own magazine using my word processor. It is called 'Wicked 91' and usually has 15 to 20 pages. Every year the name changes as the year changes. It is released every month. I send copies to all my pen pals around the country to whom I write regularly. Even though I have the biggest bedroom I still need more room!

☐ If I could have any bedroom I wanted I'd have a right big room with a big round bed. It would have a step up to it. All along one wall would be wardrobes, because I'd have loads of clothes, and there would be a big comfy chair. There would be lace and frills, everything to match and a telly, video, stereo and lots of bears. I'd have a bathroom leading off the bedroom, then I wouldn't have to dash across the landing. I'd put Sidney Poitier in my bed. I don't know what I'd do with him. Or perhaps Eddie Murphy or John Barnes, especially John Barnes.

☐ About two minutes after the voices sound Sarah stirs and turns toward me and the morning cuddling begins. As she moves, I lift my arm across the pillow and she snuggles into my breast, lifting one leg to lie over my hip. I tend to come to life quickly, she can take hours; hours that are split into tiny five minute sections. 'Just five minutes' is her equivalent of the blackbird's morning concert and equally persistent. The voices on the radio mumble on, loud enough to hear, but not to distinquish the words entirely clearly. Sarah moves position, or more truthfully, I move her, hoping to speed up her waking. I roll from my back onto my side, pulling her more closely into my breast, twining our legs together, and reaching round her soft body. 'Just five minutes,' she

whispers in response to my suggestion that if we are to be at work on time then we need to move towards the shower.

My will-power is easily overcome. After all, it's probably raining outside. Certainly, the bedroom atmosphere is colder than under the duvet, where the night's accumulation of hot air is insulating us. Besides, who would forego the chance of this stolen time together; when no pretence is needed, when, just woken from sleep, vulnerable and yet immune to the world, we can be ourselves. Two women, loving each other, sharing our dreams and strengthening their protection in order that it should carry us through another day in the real world. For getting out of bed means getting dressed, covering up, putting on the faces and bodies that the world wishes to see, losing touch with ourselves. Bed is safe. No-one intrudes here to make us odd or ill at ease. Here, surrounded by our castle of feather and foam, we are both 'Mistress of the Universe.' Small wonder that our bedroom rings with the sound of joy and laughter.

The other bedroom, the one we have for show, which is said to be mine, is a quiet sterile place. It holds no secret power to charm us, no magic to release us from the roles we play in daylight hours. Occasionally one of us has slept there, suffering from insomnia and reluctant to transmit the virus to the other. Then I feel the coldness of that room creeping between us, making a space into which emptiness and uncertainty will push their way, allowing the propriety of the world to vanquish our spontaneity. That room is cold and white, clinical, reminding me how frail the womb we create in our shared bedroom may be, and how the destructive forces of prejudice and bigotry, which seek to pull us out, kicking and screaming like new born babes are always waiting. For beds are also the places of nightmares.

☐ Our lass hates me watching her get ready on a morning because she knows I make fun of her. She stands in front of the wardrobe and starts trying on different skirts

and T-shirts. I always reckon to be asleep but I watch her through the slits in my eyes. First it's one on, then another, then something else, then she'll go back to the first. If she catches me watching her she marches off to the bathroom with an armful of clothes. She says she likes it best when I'm out so that she can have the bedroom to herself, then she can try on and take off to her heart's content.

☐   I shared a big bedroom with my sister. There was an oldfashioned brass bedstead and a marble topped wash-stand with a huge bowl and jug. One night when we were both in bed, the jug suddenly rose into the air and hovered for a few seconds until it smashed into the wall, just as though someone had picked it up and thrown it away. Of course, my mother didn't believe us when we told her what had happened so we ended up being punished for it.

☐   Getting ready to go out for the evening can be hectic in my bedroom but if I take the time to do it, it makes me feel a bit special. Glamorous, I suppose.

Ideally, I'll shower first and wash my hair. Then I put on the moisturiser. Lime green first, that makes you less ruddy. Then I do my eyes and put on the lip salve. Thank heavens for lip salve. Nail varnish can be incapacitating. I've often just lain down on the bed, a captive to drying nail varnish. Depilatory cream has caused me moments of anguish. I once went to answer the door to a man selling magazines with my legs bright pink. Raised his eyebrows that did.

The problem most of the time is deciding what to wear. I usually take the wardrobe to pieces, open all the drawers, rake out all the hangers and throw everything onto the bed. By this point, time is usually running out. That's when you find that your favourite top needs mending and your second choice needs washing. Not only that, the cat has just been sick and the phone starts to ring. Answering the phone to somebody from work whilst pretending to be fully clothed can be a lot of fun. Time is really running out now, so you end up with a compromise. The

top that's your third favourite and the trousers you were already wearing.

Coming home and taking it all off is another ritual. I'm very neat and put things away. The shoes go onto the shoe horns, the blouse back on the hanger – I usually smell it first – and the dirty knickers go straight into the Ali Baba basket.

Then when I'm in my all-in-one pyjama suit with no make-up and I look into the mirror I think, 'Is this the same person?' and I feel like Cinderella.

☐   I live in a rather small terraced house and as my daughter lives at home there is not as much space as I would like.

I like to use my bedroom as my office and workroom. I love to lie on the bed in the sunlight, writing or sorting out old photos. I keep my old photo collection in the bedroom on a shelf above my untidy writing desk. My wife is not very pleased but nobody goes in there but me so what does it matter?

☐   I love bed. It's my natural habitat and I spend a lot of time there. I work there but it's not an ideal arrangement because as soon as I wake up my word processor is there in front of me. What I want ideally is a room where I can shut the door on it all when I finish.

I heard that Roald Dahl had to get out of the house to work and so worked in his garden shed. I could do with something like that.

☐   Ours was a fraught relationship. My sister made her territorial claims and I made counter-claims. I was seriously trying to work out a way to divide the room by a curtain but the location of the windows and the positioning of the beds made that a non-starter. In the end, when we were in our teens, she moved into another room.

☐   The war was on and, when my father was fire watching, I was taken into my mother's bed to sleep. I cannot remember seeing my father naked except much later

when his body was wasted away but one night, although told not to, I peeped when my mother undressed and saw her, small breasted and silhouetted against a moonlit sky.

☐ Rain soaked the brown October afternoon. It was impossible to play outside and there wasn't much to do inside except to line up and admire the fireworks on the bedroom windowsill. They were exciting little cones and cylinders, compact, brightly coloured and closely printed with instructions about blue touchpaper. It was a good collection promising blinding flashes of light, enormous explosions of depth-charge proportions and weak-kneed terror in the timid.

'A week is a long time to wait,' said one of the boys. 'An awful long time. Perhaps we should test one. Just one − to make sure it isn't a dud. But where?'

We looked at each other and moved towards the spare bedroom, recently stripped bare of furniture, curtains and carpet. What a good place! Better still, it was a bedroom with a fireplace.

'It'll all go up the chimney, quite safe, no-one any the wiser. How very sensible.' Carefully, we balanced a Roman candle in the grate, struck a match, lit the blue touchpaper and stood back. It was a dud.

The first explosion was green and the blast knocked the firework over, pointing into the newly decorated bedroom. We could do nothing but watch, thrilled and appalled as the glare turned pink and then green, each time giving a loud bang and filling the room with coloured stars and black acrid smoke, sulphurous as hell, making us choke and panic. There was just no way of stopping it.

We tore down the stairs, out of the house, into the rain and hid.

☐ We stopped at a hotel in New York. 47 storeys up a skyscraper. The blind got stuck a bit and so my husband tried to tug it down. He pulled it and then stood frozen to the spot. The shock of standing in a window all that way up got to him.

'Don't look down, Audrey,' he stammered, 'whatever you do.'

□ It gets very noisy in the mornings in Moslem countries. The Muezzin calls us to the Mosque for prayers and your mother will run about the house shouting, 'Get up, get up, it's Aazan time.' Already people are at their businesses by 5 o'clock.

There is a lot of noise in the night in Asia as well. Sometimes people have their wedding celebrations going past your window.

□ When you're a kid, your bedroom is your world. A special place where only children are and no adults. As you get older your house swallows up that space and your bedroom becomes just another room.

□ I well remember being absent from school, confined to bed with a sore throat, and my bullying brother was made to fetch and carry for me. My bed was so high from the floor that underneath was an ideal hideaway, and not just for the fluff which feather beds seemed to produce in abundance. My brother had the bright idea of crawling underneath to scare me. When he arched his back and lifted and rolled me to the floor, my screams were heard for miles.

Alas, now beds don't have legs and there's not as much room for the dust but bed is still the most comfortable place in the house, whether for relaxation or inspiration.

□ I suppose as you get older, you start to respect your brothers' and sisters' privacy. We used to kick and tickle each other and scare each other by talking about faces at the window.

We don't do that now. I sometimes miss it.

□ My wife was a doctor and once she took me visiting across the North Road to see an old farm labourer on the Womersley Estate. The room he lived in was filthy. There were no real blankets, just a bed covered with old coats with a Lassie-come-home type dog lying on it. The only thing of any interest on the walls was a very expensive signed photograph of a grandee in Court dress. I recognised the figure immediately. It was Lord Curzon, Viceroy of India, prominent Tory politician and a man now best remembered from the rhyme:

'My name is George Nathaniel Curzon
I am a most superior purzon.'

A great intriguer, he had gallantly made his way from one high lady's bedroom to the next, politicising as he went. What his picture was doing over this poor, dirty, old bachelor's bed, I'll never know.

□ St Cecilia's and St Gabriel's were the best dorms to be in for midnight feasts at Hickleton Hall. They didn't have teachers sleeping in them and they had windows which opened on to the roof. That was important because we weren't allowed to talk in the dorms at all; if you talked you got a black mark. Everyone owned up if they spoke. It didn't matter if the teachers weren't there. God would know. When you got out of the windows in St Cecilia's or St Gabriel's you were on the flat roof over the entrance porch and you wouldn't have to own up to talking there. It was speaking in the dormitory which was forbidden.

Word went round before high tea if there was to be a midnight feast. We'd always have one when there was a visitor in the dorm, a girl who'd just come to the school, or occasionally, we'd do it for someone's birthday. We'd do it two or three times a term.

Once it was decided, everyone had to save an extra slice of the thick white bread which was served for tea with jam and butterballs. One or two had the temerity to call them marge balls which is what they were. You folded your doorstep in half, looked round to make sure none of the nuns or Miss Mitchell was watching and then tucked the sandwich between your white knicker lining and your navy blue serge outer knicker. After tea there was prep, then biscuits and orange juice and

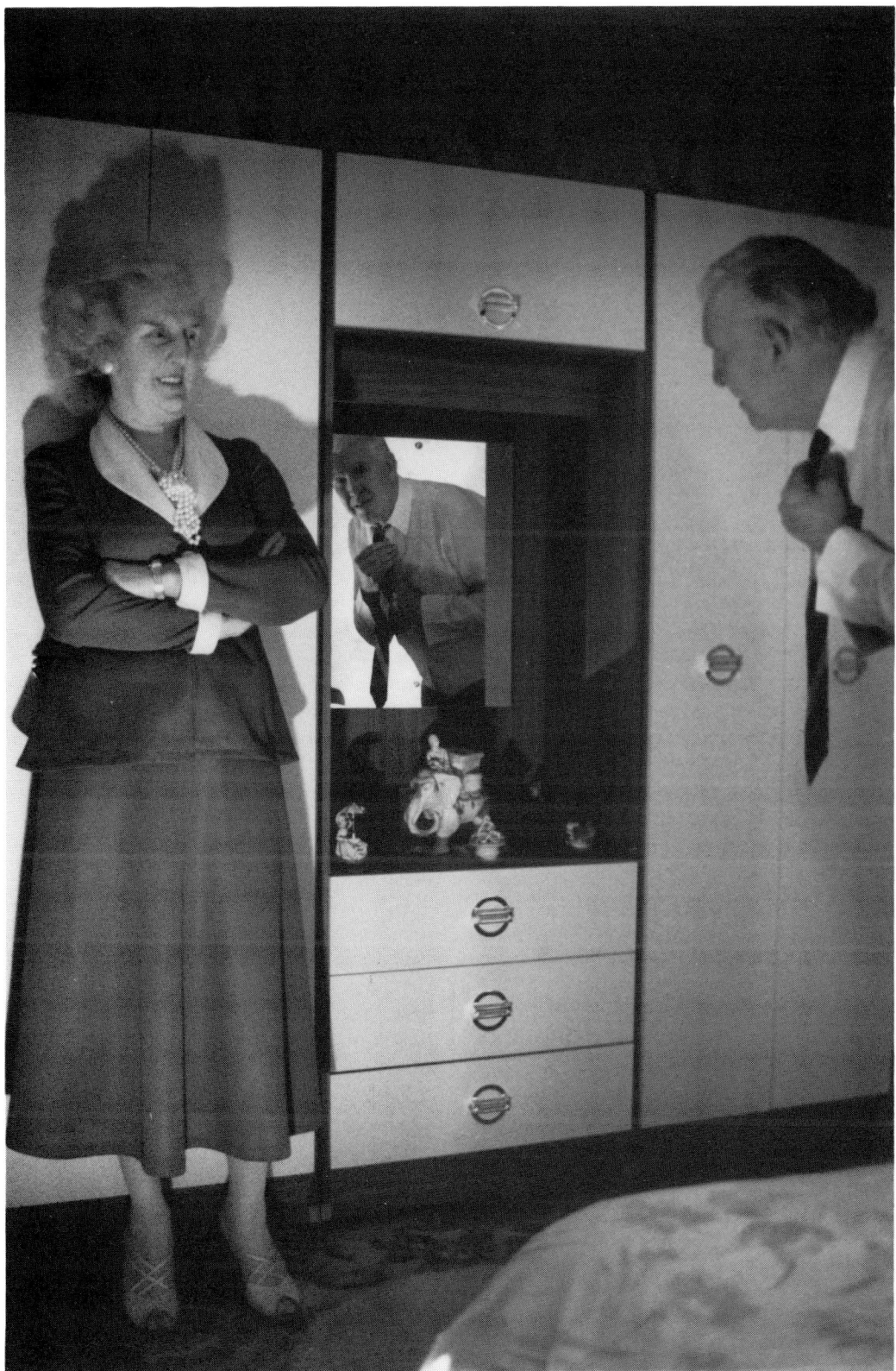

then we were allowed to go into the marble hall and play jacks or pick-a-sticks till bedtime. If you were prepared to risk being seen you saved your biscuit too.

At some point after supper you pretended you needed the loo and hoped you weren't directed to the ones on the Great North Road or Watling Street corridors. Then you could go to one of the upstairs loos and with a palpitating heart nip along into the dormitory to put the sandwich in your bedside locker. It was terrifying having the evidence on you. Once the food was safe in your locker you had to eat up all the crumbs that fell to the floor in case they gave you away. That's why only the brave ones took biscuits; biscuits crumbled easily whereas bread went into a solid damp piece in your knicker leg. Some girls even managed to get orange juice up to the dormitory but I never found out how they concealed it.

At the end of prep Judith Ramsey, the Form Monitor, went round surreptiously asking everybody if they'd been to the lavatory properly. I thought it meant had you pulled the chain properly so I always said yes but I noticed some people said no and were led away. One night curiosity overcame me and I said no just to see what happened to them. I was led down Great North Road to the surgery and left in a queue at the door. When I got to the front of the queue I was given a tablespoon of syrup of figs. It was totally disgusting. I assumed it was a punishment for not pulling the chain properly.

When you finally got to bed you had to make sure you stayed awake till Compline. All the Sisters, the Tertiaries, the Novices, the Deaconess, Miss Mitchell, everyone, disappeared off to the chapel for the Compline service. Compline gave us fifteen minutes of freedom.

It took two of us to pull up the sash window. Outside the window was a ledge which you weren't sure would hold your weight the first time you stepped on it and then you were on the roof and could run about or go and look down the beautiful glass dome into the entrance hall. You'd

halve your sandwich with someone who hadn't been able to get one and a bottle of orange juice was passed round. Since the nuns shared communion wine we reckoned we could share the same bottle. But the food wasn't that important — it was the fun of running about barefoot in your nightie with lots of other nine year old girls.

We were never caught. Once, a girl said that Sister Bridget Mary and a visitor were down in the entrance hall when she'd looked through the dome. We didn't know whether to believe her or not. I was not one who dared to look down again to see if they were there.

You could follow the progress of Compline by the various bells that were rung. When the last bell started to toll we'd all jump back into bed with loads of giggling and panic.

It always seemed a very long wait, lying in bed and keeping awake for the midnight feast, although Compline was at a quarter to nine. Some idiots couldn't contain their giggling and used to stuff sheets in their mouths to suppress it. I thought they were stupid to jeopardise everything. Most of all I remember curling up in bed afterwards, always with wet feet.

☐   In my first year at University, I had a room in college and discovered the delights of sex. I still had a soft spot for home rituals though, so come Shrove Tuesday I decided to make pancakes. I couldn't quite remember how my mum did it so I had to follow a recipe in a library book. After you'd mixed the batter it said, 'Leave to stand overnight in a cool place.' Well, college rooms, like hospitals, are always overheated and although there was a tiny kitchen with two hotplates there was no fridge. Most students stuck their perishables in a carrier bag and hung them on a string out the window. I couldn't very well do that with a bowlful of batter.

Study bedrooms were small but they had everything crammed in them — bed, desk, drawers, wardrobe, armchair and even, at one end, a washbasin. I decided to fill the washbasin with cold water and stand the bowl in that. It worked fine and we forgot about it. At two in the morning after a particularly sticky session, my boyfriend heaved himself off the bed, groped his way to the washbasin and dunked his cock in a bowl of batter.

☐ At Carr Hall a whole sign language came into being because we weren't allowed to speak in the dormitory. We had a symbol for every Sister. Sister Eileen was small so you indicated that; for Sister Ingrid you went Ingrid Stringrid and made a sign like a piece of string.

If you did speak you had to own up and go to the Dormitory Meeting where you'd be given 20 lines of Shakespeare to learn. A week later you had to go to the next Dormitory Meeting and recite them. Regular offenders became very good at memorising Shakespeare. It was an act of bravado to see how near to the Dormitory Meeting you could get without opening the book. Once, for a dare, I managed to learn the entire passage while I was waiting in the queue.

We also communicated in a written form, especially between dormitories. You could lean out of the window and float little messages along the gutter. 'I love you, darling, I'd like to kiss you in the Music Room.' It was very exciting. If a gust of wind came along the messages could blow off out of the gutter into the rose garden where they might be seen by the Sisters coming out of Compline.

☐ Two students I was at college with ate fish and chips in bed every Friday night. It was a ritual to go to the pub and get fairly drunk, then call at the chip shop, dash home and leap into bed to eat the fish and chips as a prelude to sex. I discovered this when half a dozen of us followed on to their house after the pub, when they weren't expecting us.

It was a bedsit in a Victorian house in Aberdeen with no heating. The paint was filthy, the carpet was mouldy and, apart from a single armchair, the double bed was the only furniture. It was an enormous bed, the sort you could park a car underneath, it was so far off the ground. Jane and Robert were naked on it with everything − blankets, duffel coats, clothing − piled on top of them to keep warm. He was a big hairy bloke and she was small and spherical with long black hair. They had a large Cerebos salt drum which he decanted a useable amount from into his belly-button − a small oasis where no hair grew − and they both dipped into it.